THE
GREATEST
OF
THESE

Books by J. D. Jones

The Apostles of Jesus

Commentary on Mark

The Greatest of These

The Hope of the Gospel

The J. D. Jones Classic Library

THE GREATEST OF THESE

*Expository Sermons
on 1 Corinthians 13*

J. D. JONES

Grand Rapids, MI 49501

The Greatest of These by J. D. Jones

Published in 1995 by Kregel Publications, a division of Kregel, Inc., P.O. Box 2607, Grand Rapids, MI 49501. Kregel Publications provides trusted, biblical publications for Christian growth and service. Your comments and suggestions are valued.

Cover and Book Design: Alan G. Hartman

Library of Congress Cataloging-in-Publication Data
Jones, J. D. (John Daniel), 1865–1942.
   The greatest of these / by J. D. Jones.
     p. cm.
   Originally published: London: Hodder and Stoughton, 1925.
   1. Bible, N.T. Corinthians, 1st XIII—Sermons.
2. Love—Biblical teaching. I. Title.
BS2675.4.J66   1995   241'.4—dc20   95-13295
                                            CIP

ISBN 0-8254-2974-9 (paperback)

1 2 3 4 5 Printing / Year 99 98 97 96 95

Printed in the United States of America

Contents

Preface

I have only the usual reason—or excuse—for publishing these sermons: many of my own people who heard them preached wished to possess them in more permanent form. They were preached in the course of my regular ministry, and they are printed exactly as they were preached. I am indebted to many writers and thinkers, several I have mentioned by name in the succeeding pages. I wish, however, to express here my special indebtedness to the late Dr. Thomas Charles Edwards, whose massive commentary was never out of my hands.

The actual preparation of the book for the press, the reading of the proofs, and so forth, has been undertaken entirely by my friend and colleague the Reverend J. Gwilym Jones. Without his help the book would never have seen the light.

My prayer is that this little volume may not only help to a fuller understanding of the chapter of which it treats, but may also prove of some religious comfort and help to its readers.

CHAPTER ONE

The Hymn of Love

And a still more excellent way shew I unto you.
—1 Corinthians 12:31

The thirteenth chapter of 1 Corinthians—Paul's great hymn on love—is, like the Twenty-third Psalm, one of those passages of Scripture which the preacher hesitates to touch lest by clumsy handling he should impair its beauty. And yet—again like the Twenty-third Psalm—while it daunts the preacher it also fascinates him and challenges him. For while something of its exquisite beauty reveals itself to us at the very first reading or hearing, there are glories and little intimate delicacies in it which only reveal themselves as we allow our minds to brood and ponder over it. To it that word from the Old Testament may be truly applied, "the stones thereof are the place of sapphires, and it has dust of gold." Every preacher who has discovered some of the wealth of this chapter naturally wants to share it with his people, and so throughout the thirty-five years of my ministry I have cherished the intention of preaching a short series of sermons upon this familiar chapter. Up to now, however, I have never passed beyond the "intending" stage. But now, at length, I am going to be bold enough to ask you to explore with me the wealthy content of this exquisite hymn.

There is a further difficulty which the preacher has to face who intends to make this chapter his theme, which does not confront him even when he preaches on the Twenty-third Psalm. Not only are the verses themselves among the most familiar and beautiful in the whole of Sacred Writ, but they have been made the subject of one of the most popular booklets ever written. Professor Henry Drummond was a great religious influence in his day and he published more than one book that had an immense vogue. His *Natural Law in the Spiritual World* and his *Ascent of Man* were books that greatly affected the preaching of thirty years ago.

But not even those famous books attained the popularity of the booklet he published entitled *The Greatest Thing in the World*. That is not surprising, because while the other books, *Natural Law* and *The Ascent of Man*, are more or less scientific and ask for a mind more or less trained, *The Greatest Thing in the World* is addressed frankly *ad populum*. And the people gave it a mighty welcome. It has been sold by the hundred thousand—my own copy is in the 350th thousand; it has been translated into all kinds of languages. It is quite easily the most widely read of modern religious books and has attained a popularity reminding one almost of Bunyan's *Pilgrim's Progress*. And *The Greatest Thing in the World* is simply an exposition of this thirteenth chapter of 1 Corinthians—an exposition characterized by all Drummond's insight and freshness and charm of style. The chapters were originally given, I believe, as addresses at the Summer Conference at Northfield. In their printed form they have become the cherished and prized possession of multitudes of Christian folk. I have no doubt that during these Sunday mornings I shall be speaking to many who are familiar with the little volume; I dare say the mere fact that I am preaching on the chapter will cause many of you to take up the little volume afresh in order to refresh your memories of Drummond's exposition. And that constitutes the special additional difficulty which confronts any preacher who proposes to lecture on this chapter. He has not only the familiarity of the chapter to contend with, but he has also to face the fact that his people are already well acquainted with the best commentary on this chapter that ever has been written or perhaps ever can be written. To preach without being a slavish imitator of Drummond and reproducing in feebler language what he has so exquisitely said is the special difficulty which confronts the preacher who makes this chapter his theme. And yet I am going to venture. I do not suppose I shall say anything new. I am quite sure that I cannot add anything to the beauty and power of the chapter—that would be to expect to be able to gild what is already pure gold. But it may be that as we study its verses together we may discover in it beauties and glories that had hitherto escaped us, so that this chapter, rich and beautiful as we now know it to be, may become to us richer and more beautiful still.

In this sermon I shall do little more than say a few words by way of introduction. And the first fact to which I wish to call attention is this—this great lyric in praise of love comes to us from the pen of Paul.

Paul As the Apostle of Love

Usually we regard John as being par excellence, the Apostle of Love. Love is the keynote of his epistles. This is the way in which he describes God for us—God is Love. This is how he sums up our duty to one another: "Beloved, let us love one another." The word was ever upon John's lips. There is a beautiful legend that says that in extreme old age he was carried for the last time into the meeting place of the Christians at Ephesus to give them a kind of farewell message, and these were the faltering words that fell from his lips: "Little children, love one another." *Love* was emphatically John's word. In contrast with John, Paul is usually regarded as the great preacher of faith. "By grace are ye saved, through faith." That is the great message we identify with Paul. The core of his gospel was this, that forgiveness is not earned, it is not merited, but it is given freely to the man who takes God at His word, who humbly believes the great message of Christ's Cross. Perhaps we are not far wrong in saying that the two apostles do differ in their emphasis—that John does specially emphasize love and Paul does specially emphasize faith, but we go completely astray if we make an antithesis between the apostles as if the one emphasized love to the exclusion of faith, and the other emphasized faith to the exclusion of love. If John emphasizes love it is not that he doesn't acknowledge the importance of faith. Listen to this from him: "This is the victory which overcometh the world, even our faith." While as for St. Paul, while his gospel centers in the declaration that salvation comes by faith, he is just as emphatic as St. John in insisting upon the importance of love. He says in one place that "love is the fulfilling of the law." There would be no need for any other law if men obeyed the law of love. Everyone would give to God His due, if he loved Him. Everyone would give to his brother his due, if he loved him. There is no need to tell a man who loves his father and mother to honor them. He does it naturally and inevitably.

And it would be preposterous, as Drummond says, to tell him not to kill. "You could only insult him if you suggested that he should not steal—how could he steal from those he loved? It would be superfluous to beg him not to bear false witness against his neighbor: if he loved him, it would be the last thing he would do. And you would never dream of urging him not to covet his neighbor's goods. He would rather he possessed the goods than himself." Love worketh no ill to his neighbor, Paul says. On the contrary, it always seeks his good. Therefore it is the one duty that sums up and includes every other duty. We could expunge every law from our statute book—laws would be effete, superfluous, unnecessary—if only men loved one another. Love, for the happy conduct of life, is the one thing needful, says St. Paul. It is "the fulfilling of the Law." John himself never said a greater thing about love than that. And it is the same apostle Paul who wrote this hymn—the noblest description of love and the finest eulogy of love ever penned. And in it he deliberately sets love even above faith. In one of its opening sentences he declares that though he have all faith so as to remove mountains, but have not love, he is nothing. And in the last sentence of the hymn he declares that the three abiding treasures are faith, hope, love—and then, as if for a moment he had been weighing their respective values in his mind, he adds this, "and the greatest of these is love." So perhaps Drummond is not far out of it in characterizing love as being, not simply in the judgment of John but also in the judgment of Paul, "the greatest thing in the world."

"And this," says F. W. Robertson, "is an arrangement of God's Providence, for if the apostle Paul had exalted the grace of faith only and the apostle John that of love only, we might have conceived that each magnified especially his own gift and that his judgment was guided by his peculiar temperament." But as it is we see each apostle emphasizing the thing for which the other specially stood. There is no schism or division among the Bible writers. There is no vital difference between John and Paul, between Peter and James. They preach the Gospel with their own distinctive accents, they approach it from their own points of view—but they all proclaim the same essential Gospel, and they all declare the same central truth.

The Word Love

I pass on now to say a word or two about that love which is the subject of this glorious hymn. The word Paul uses for love is the word ἀγάπη. Now this is not the common or usual word for love. On the contrary, it is never found in classical Greek writings, though the verb ἀγαπάω is not unknown. The word ἀγάπη is born, Archbishop Trench says, "within the bosom of revealed religion." The Greek language was rich in words descriptive of love in one or other of its various aspects. But the word in common and general use was the word ἔρως. Now why did not the New Testament writers employ the word which was in common and regular use? Why go out of their way to coin a new word which must have sounded unfamiliar and strange? The reason undoubtedly is this—that the word ἔρως had become, as Archbishop Trench again says, so steeped in sensual passion and carried with it such an atmosphere of unholiness that the truth of God abstained from any defiling contact with it. The most superficial acquaintance with Greek literature is sufficient to make one realize the truth of what the Archbishop says. Ἔρως in Greek, like *amour* in French, had become corrupt to its core. It was inseparably associated with the idea of physical passion. It was scarcely to be distinguished from lust. It was because it was thus soaked in impurity that the Christian writers shrank from the use of it even though it meant having to coin a new word of their own. For the love which they inculcated—the love that was due to God, and the love that was due to man—was a pure and holy and exalted thing. There was a suggestion even of austerity about it. It was love with reverence in it. It was not a sensuous and sensual thing at all. It was an intellectual-spiritual thing. It was a thing of the mind and the soul as well as of the heart. There are some commentators who profess regret that the apostles didn't lay hold of the word ἔρως, besmirched and corrupted as it was, and cleanse it of the filth that had accumulated upon it and reconsecrate it to pure and noble use. But the word was so deeply degraded, the idea of fleshly desire was so deeply ingrained in it, that the apostles felt it was probably past saving. Anyhow, in a society so honeycombed with immorality as was that in which Christianity made its first appearance, if love was to be emphasized as the supreme grace, it was essential that it should be made perfectly clear that it was love of a different kind from that which formed the subject of Greek plays, that it was a pure, beautiful, austere, and exalted thing to which no touch of grossness attached itself. And this the apostles did by the adoption of this new word ἀγάπη. I am not sure that the word *love* does not need to be rescued afresh in these days of ours. It has been debased and degraded by our modern writers until it has sunk almost as low as the Greek ἔρως. The love of passion and of sensual desire is the only love they seem to recognize. They give it a mean, vulgar origin. Love to them is simply the expression of the sexual instinct. It is a physical thing, not a thing of the mind and the soul. And love so interpreted becomes not the greatest and best thing in the world, but a blight and a miasma and a devastation. It degrades womanhood, it is the ruin of the home, it is a curse upon children, and it lands us in the morals of the sty. We need to rescue the very idea of love. We ought to give things their proper names and not prostitute great words by applying them to base, unholy things. Vagrant, sensual desire is not love. Its proper name is lust. Love is a pure and holy thing—white as the driven snow. It is a sacred and beautiful thing. The test of genuine love is this—can we give it to God? For ἀγάπη is the feeling we are to cherish towards God as well as the feeling we are to cherish towards men. There is a great element of reverence and awe in love, and where there is no reverence there is no real love. It would clarify our moral judgments if we were more careful in our use of words. We can make an ugly thing seem fair by flinging over it the garment of a beautiful word. This age has done that with this sacred word *love*. It has used the word to make things inherently vile seem specious and fair. Its effect is to confuse the moral judgment, and the confusion of moral judgment may easily issue in moral disaster. We need to rescue the word and jealously to guard its honor. This is love, this greatest thing in the world which the apostle here describes, this beautiful and holy thing which suffereth long and is kind—which thinketh no evil and rejoiceth not in iniquity but rejoiceth in the truth—this and not the sensual and vagrant passion to which the modern novelist applies the name. Love is a holy and sacred thing. It does not identify us with the brute, it unites us with God. "Love is of God and every one that loveth is born of God and knoweth God."

The Context

And the final introductory word which I wish to speak this morning has reference to the context and the occasion which prompted this lyric outburst. You notice I have quoted as my text the last clause of chapter 12. I did so because this exquisite hymn of love sprang really out of the discussion in chapter 12. The discussion in that chapter gathers round the question of "spiritual gifts." The Corinthian Christians seem to have been specially richly endowed with *carismata*. They were of various kinds—prophecy, the gift of tongues, the interpretation of tongues and so on. It was this "diversity" of gifts that gave rise to the trouble. For the members were disposed every one to exalt his own special gift to the disparagement of the gift bestowed upon his brother. The church, as a result, seethed with jealousy and envy. And I gather from the letter that the rivalry was particularly keen as between the people who had the gift of "prophecy"—the gift of preaching as we would say—and those who had the gift of "tongues," a kind of ecstatic speech which was unintelligible to the ordinary hearer unless there was present someone who could interpret. People are prone to reserve their admiration for the bizarre and the extraordinary and the abnormal. And so the Corinthians were inclined to give their admiration to these people who spoke with tongues, rather than to those who had the more commonplace but more profitable gift of prophecy. That was the precise situation with which Paul is dealing in chapter 12. He tries to reason the Corinthians out of this foolish and sinful jealousy by reminding them that all gifts are necessary to the full life of the church, and that it is as absurd for one man to envy another as it would be for the foot to envy the hand or the ear the eye. All the members are necessary to the health and completeness of the body, and all the different spiritual gifts are wanted for the full vigor and health of the church. And he finishes his argument by bidding them all desire earnestly the "greater" gifts, not necessarily the more showy and surprising, but the gifts that will contribute most to the edification of the church.

And just at that point, when he has completed his argument, it strikes the apostle that there is something better even than the greater gifts, and that there is a much surer way of banishing envy and securing unity than the thought of mutual benefit which he has been pressing upon them. And so he adds this sentence: "And a still more excellent way shew I unto you." And then follows this glorious hymn on love. Love is the grace which is better than the greatest of gifts, better than tongues, better than prophecy, better than faith, better than philanthropy, better even than sacrificial courage. And love is the more excellent way by which unity of heart and mind is to be achieved. It is this latter thought that is the more prominent in the sentence of my text though in the chapter itself the superiority of love as a means to an end is lost sight of in the glowing panegyric the apostle pronounces on love itself.

For just a moment then, let me dwell upon the thought which

the sentence of my text suggests. Love is the more excellent way, says the apostle. But the way to what? One of the greatest commentators on this epistle says that what the apostle means is that love is a more excellent way to the attainment of gifts than eagerness of emulation. It is not through the exercise of gifts we attain to love; it is love that develops the gifts within us. To seek the "greater gifts" may be a good thing; to seek love is a better thing. To cultivate talents and powers is a good thing; but to cultivate the spirit of helpful and sacrificial love is the best of all. And the Christian is out not for any second best, but for the best of all.

All that is true. But I cannot help feeling that the thought of unity is uppermost in the apostle's mind. The whole argument of the chapter has been an argument meant to foster unity. He has urged it on the ground that the gifts of each are for the good of all, and that all profit by the gifts of each. When this fact of interdependence and mutual profit is really grasped, envy and jealousy become simply foolish and stupid. It is an argument addressed to, shall I say, the common sense of the Corinthians, and it is conclusive enough in its way. And yet I think that at the end of it Paul felt it would not produce the unity he desired. At any rate he knew there was a much more effective means of securing unity than by arguments addressed to the practical wisdom of people—and that was by getting them really to love one another. And so at the conclusion of his long argument he says "And a still more excellent way shew I unto you"—and this more excellent way is just the golden pathway of love. Love will succeed where common sense and expediency hopelessly fail. Love is the cement that binds the loose stones into a building; love is the ligament which binds the members into a body. It is the one force potent enough to create and secure unity. There are differences between children in a home, but there is no envy or jealousy; the children love one another, and love knits them into a united family.

Love is everywhere the secret of unity. It is the way to *unity in society.* Common sense ought to teach us that we are members one of another and we can prosper only as we serve one another. But common sense has entirely failed to bind the various classes together. They face one another in something like hostile array. Class antagonizes class, and some deluded or evil people seem to think the millennium is going to be furthered by class war. And in the meantime the whole community suffers. Various expedients have been devised to promote cooperation. I am not disparaging them. No doubt they help to alleviate the trouble. But there is only one way to real unity and that is the way of love. Society will be one when men learn to love one another and in love to minister to one another.

It is the same with *international unity*. We have been taught by bitter experience the tragic cost of war. We are reaping throughout the world the ugly fruit of discord and strife. In the interests of our own happiness and prosperity we want international peace. Common sense and expediency would urge us to it. In spite of the League of Nations, in spite of treaties and alliances, Europe is in a state of tension at this hour. The fact of it is none of these prudential expedients will avail to banish war. The disarmament needed is a disarmament of the mind. The real security is not a rectification of frontiers but a change of spirit. Let people learn to love one another in Christ and they can afford to beat their swords into plowshares and their spears into pruninghooks, for there will be "abundance of peace till the moon be no more."

And to come back to what was chiefly in the apostle's mind—love is the secret of *unity in the church*, in the local community and in the church in the great sense. The church as we know it is rent and torn by division. Common sense bids us unite, for division means weakness and our schisms and antagonisms give the Enemy cause to blaspheme. Yet here we are divided into a number of competing if not hostile camps. The folly and sin of our disunion has come home to many serious minds, and they are exploring the possibilities of drawing the scattered members of Christ's flock together. Again I have no criticism to pass upon their efforts; I say Godspeed to them. But there is a better and surer way than that of ecclesiastical *rearrangement*—and that is the way of love. We shall be joined into a blessed unity when we learn to love one another. And where shall we learn to love? Where but in Christ? When we stand before His Cross and realize we all share in that common salvation—that the sacrifice there offered and the love there shown was as much for the Romanist as for the Protestant, as much for the Anglican as for the Free churchman, shall we not be compelled to say, "Beloved, if God so love us, we ought also to love one another." That is the real hope of unity—not by way of identity of thought, nor by way of identity of organization—but by the more excellent way of a common love. So this might well be our prayer:

In every land, in every home,
In every heart let love increase;
Let love proclaim Thy kingdom come,
O reign among us, Prince of peace.

CHAPTER TWO

Love's Excellence

*Though I speak with the tongues of men and of angels
and have not love, I am become as sounding brass or a
clanging cymbal. And though I have the gift of
prophecy, and know all mysteries and all knowledge;
and though I have all faith so as to remove mountains,
but have not love, I am nothing. And though I bestow all
my goods to feed the poor, and though I give my body to
be burned, but have not love, it profiteth me nothing.*
—1 Corinthians 13:1–3

"Yet shew I you a more excellent way." That is the last sentence which the apostle's pen had written. He had been pointing out to the Corinthians that it was a foolish and suicidal thing to let jealousy of one another's gifts breed dissension in the church. He had been urging upon them that all these various gifts were as necessary to the health and vigor of the church as the various organs—eye and ear, and hand and foot—are to the efficiency and welfare of the body. And just because each gift was necessary, jealousy of this or the other gift, or contempt of the less showy gifts was sheer stupidity. There is no escape from the apostle's argument. It is just plain, straightforward, but absolutely convincing common sense. And then it came home to the apostle that considerations of mutual profit might after all entirely fail to secure the desired unity: that common sense might not avail to solve the problem. At any rate, there was a much more certain path to unity, a much more sure method of banishing dissension than considerations of mutual profit could supply. The real remedy was that these Corinthian Christians should love one another. Love is the ligament that can bind the members of a church to one another and make a "body" of them. This was "the more excellent way" which he had in his mind when he penned that last sentence of chapter 12. And what we should naturally have expected after such a sentence is that Paul should proceed to show how love would succeed where common sense might wholly fail. But what he does is to break out into an impassioned, glorious eulogy of love itself. It is as if at the mere thought of love the apostle had become so absorbed and engrossed in the beauty of the thing itself that he clean forgot for the moment all about the end to the realization of which love was to be the means. There is a suggestive little touch in the story of the Samaritan woman at Jacob's well. Apparently it was a long way from her house to the well, for one of the advantages of the stranger's promise of living water would be that she would not every day have to trudge "all the way hither to draw." Water was a necessity, and every day she walked that weary stretch of country to get it. It was for water she had come on this particular day. But she found something better than water—she found her Lord. And this is the suggestive little touch in the narrative, "she left her water pot." In her absorption in Jesus, in her joy at discovering her Lord, she forgot all about the errand that had brought her to the well. "She left her water pot." It was very much like that with St. Paul. He had intended to go on to show how love was the real way to unity. But as soon as ever the vision of love presents itself to his imagination he forgets all about his original intention and pours out this rapturous hymn in praise of love itself.

Paul starts, if I may so express it, on the top note. He begins with a magnificent fortissimo. When as a young man of twenty-three John Clifford delivered his first speech to the Baptist Union, the delegates who heard him said that it was not so much a speech as a shout. Well, the apostle begins his hymn with a glorious shout! The Corinthians had been quarrelling about gifts—wrangling as to which was greatest, whether tongues or prophecy, or miracles, and all the while they had been leaving the greatest gift of all entirely out of account. Tongues and miracles and prophecy were nothing as compared to love. Love was the supreme thing and without it no other gift was worth anything at all. Listen to him: "Though I speak with the tongues of men and of angels and have not love, I am become as sounding brass or a clanging cymbal; and though I have the gift of prophecy and understand all mysteries and all knowledge; and though I have all faith so as to remove mountains and have not love, I am nothing. And though I bestow all my goods to feed the poor and though I give my body to be burned and have not love, it profiteth me nothing." It is not simply the absolute supremacy of love the apostle is asserting here; he says that every other gift derives its value from it, and that all other gifts are worthless without it. I read in one of the London papers the other day an article by one woman on the place of love in life. And the point the good woman made—with obvious satisfaction to herself—was that whereas in the Victorian era love had been the whole of a woman's life, now it had become a mere "adjunct." Love an adjunct! Love a sort of minor interest! Now woman had got her work and her freedom, and her franchise, and love was relegated to its proper place! Well, if the Victorians interpreted love as being the whole of life—at any rate they had the great apostle on their side. Look at these opening verses! Love is no adjunct to the apostle. It is no minor interest. It is not something that competes for place with work and politics and play. It is the thing that gives everything else value. It is the thing that confers upon everything else its worth. The gifts Paul mentions in these verses were not insignificant and commonplace gifts. They were the greatest and most coveted of gifts. And what he says of them all is that they are valueless without love. They are like a row of zeros without a digit in front to give them value. Write down a row of zeros. Write down a dozen of them, and what do they amount to? Exactly nothing! And if you were to write a thousand of them they would be nothing still. But put a figure in front of those zeros and they at once become significant. They stand for something, they mean much. Put three zeros down and they amount to nothing. Just a 1 in front of them and they mean a thousand. And it is like that with gifts and powers, says the apostle. They count for nothing without love. Life itself is nothing without love. It is no mere adjunct, no mere minor interest. It is that which makes life significant and worthwhile; it is that which lends to every gift its worth. Let us look at some of the illustrations wherewith the apostle enforces this truth.

Eloquence

He begins with that gift of tongues, which of all gifts the Corinthians coveted most. It was apparently a kind of ecstatic speech understood neither by the speaker nor by his audience unless there happened to be an interpreter present. It was, however, a much admired gift because it was so strange and showy. Let me this morning, however, treat eloquence as being the modern equivalent of this "gift of tongues." Now, eloquence is a great and noble gift. To be able to rouse, to calm, to persuade, to convict men is a mighty and magnificent endowment. And of all kinds of eloquence, the gift of sacred eloquence is the noblest and most splendid gift of all. I have listened to great preachers. I have heard them melt and sway men. I have heard Joseph Parker leave people absolutely stunned and breathless by the sheer force of his speech. I have seen my own countrymen break into uncontrollable emotion beneath the subduing eloquence of Herber Evans. That gift of eloquence dedicated to noble ends, used to stir men to noble living and to win them for Christ, is a great and splendid gift. It is one of those "excellent gifts" that I covet. And yet, says the apostle, a man may speak with the tongues of men and of angels, that is, he may have the gift of eloquence carried to its sublimest pitch but if he have not love, he becomes sounding brass or a clanging cymbal. And what the apostle means by that is that eloquence without love is so much empty, meaningless, ineffective noise. There is no real eloquence without love. The Corinthians coveted this gift of tongues because they imagined it exalted them in the eyes of their fellows. It was a showy gift. And they exercised it for their own self-glorification. They gave no thought to the profit of their fellow members. They thought only of their own pride. And the apostle says speech inspired by such motives is as empty as sounding brass. It is love alone that can make speech mighty. The truth holds good to this day. A man may have a great command of speech, he may be a master of epigram, he may spin fine-sounding sentences and weave cunning sequences; at the finish his speech may be limp and empty and ineffective. What is it lends power and effectiveness to speech? Is it not the conviction and passion of the speaker? And what are conviction and passion but the effects of love? A man must be in love with his theme if he is to speak effectively upon it. Passion, soul—they constitute the power of speech, and they are the product of love. That is why many a speech, full of literary beauty and rhetorically perfect, leaves an audience cold. And halting, broken speech, suffused with the fire of a great passion, kindles an audience to white heat. And all this is specially true of speech about sacred things. The condition of power is love to God and man. That is what preaching means—speech inspired by a great passion born of a mighty love. The mere gift of words does not make a preacher; the power to state a case does not make a preacher; the ability to give an interesting talk does not make a preacher. They are all gifts that are valuable in a preacher's equipment, but the one absolutely vital thing is that people should feel that burning, flaming through every sentence is the fire of a mighty love. "The love of Christ constraineth me," said one of the greatest preachers who ever lived. It was that love, throbbing in all his speech, that gave it power to melt and subdue human hearts. "I should have painted Him much better if I had loved Him more," said Gustav Dore' about a figure of Christ that stood upon his easel. And let every preacher lay the truth to heart: that the deeper and more ardent the love, the more mighty the speech. But if there is no love we might just as well give up and keep silent. People have a curious power of recognizing when a man is speaking because it is his duty, and when he speaks because he cannot help it, because his heart is aflame. And once they suspect a man is preaching as a matter of business he may be ever so eloquent, but his effect upon them is nil. "If I speak with the tongues of men and of angels but have not love, I am become as sounding brass or a clanging cymbal."

Prophecy and Faith

In illustration of his thesis, the apostle considers next the gifts of prophecy and faith. There is not the slightest doubt that he himself laid far more store by the gift of prophecy than he did by the gift of tongues. Prophecy ministered to the profit of the hearer—while tongues simply expressed the speaker's own ecstasy. Prophecy is not to be understood as a forecasting of the future. It corresponds more to our preaching. Men who had insight into spiritual truth uttered what they knew, for the comfort and inspiration of their fellow worshippers. Paul valued this gift almost above every other. That is why at the close of chapter 14, he says that while he does not forbid the speaking with tongues, he exhorts the Corinthians to "desire earnestly to prophesy." But prophecy—precious as the gift is and the spiritual insight out of which it springs and the faith which it proclaims is all worthless without love. "Though I have the gift of prophecy and know all mysteries and all knowledge; and though I have all faith, so as to remove mountains, and have not love, I am nothing." You notice what the apostle says, a man may possess the gifts of prophecy and knowledge and faith and yet himself be nothing. The gifts are significant. They are useful. By his preaching he may help others; by his knowledge he may enrich others; by his faith he may strengthen others; yet for lack of love he himself may be nothing. It is not gifts that count with God but character, and the foundation of the Christian character is love. A man may have all manner of gifts, but if he has not love he is in God's sight just nothing at all. "He that loveth not, knoweth not God, for God is love." Loveless prophets, loveless seers, loveless believers—can there be such beings? Apparently there may. I read, for example, of some people who said, "Lord, Lord, did we not prophesy in Thy Name?" And the Lord's terrible reply is this: "I never knew you; depart from me, ye that work iniquity." They had the gift of prophecy, but they had not love, and therefore Christ did not reckon them as His own. Loveless faith—can there be such a thing? Yes, apparently there can. John and James had faith in Jesus— but one day they wanted to call down fire from heaven to destroy a certain Samaritan village through which they passed. They had faith, but at the time they had not much love, and Jesus addressed to them the solemn warning: "Ye know not what spirit ye are of." Loveless faith—it has been accountable for some tragic pages in the history of the Christian church. What are all the religious persecutions but illustrations of this very thing, loveless faith? The men who lit the fires of Smithfield for Protestant confessors had in their way faith enough. They had a real—even if mistaken—zeal for religion. They thought that in burning heretics they were really doing God service. It was faith of a kind, but there was no love in it. And the religious controversies through which we often pass illustrate the same thing. It is quite right to contend earnestly for the faith, but there is something wrong when in our contention we become harsh and venomous and bitter—and it is proverbial that there are no controversies so fierce and angry as religious controversies. It will be no excuse or defense to say that it was the faith we fought for if we transgressed the law of love. Love is the one thing needful. Love is the link that binds us to God. Love is the quality that proclaims we belong to the divine family. We may have all kinds of brilliant and dazzling gifts—prophecy, insight, faith—but if we haven't love, we are nothing. Christ will not recognize us for His own. It is not what we have but what we are that really matters. It is not our gifts but our character that counts. "Though I have the gift of prophecy and know all mysteries and all knowledge, and though I have all faith so as to remove mountains and have not love, I am nothing."

Giving

And for a third and final illustration of his theme the apostle takes into consideration the matter of giving, culminating in the supreme sacrifice of life. And he finds again that these are worthless without love. "And though I bestow all my goods to feed the poor, and though I give my body to be burned, but have not love, it profiteth me nothing." Now, the grace of giving is a great Christian virtue. The New Testament has a great deal to say about it. I do not think I am going too far when I say that our Lord makes it the test of entrance into the glory and blessedness of heaven. In that great judgment scene which we get in Matthew 25, the people who are summoned to inherit the kingdom are the people who fed the hungry, clothed the naked, visited the sick, while the people who are told to "depart" into the outer darkness are the people who failed to discharge any of these offices of helpful ministry. I read again in the Gospel of St. Luke that Dives lifted up his eyes, being in torment because he neglected the beggar Lazarus who lay in his sores at his very gate. And the reason for making the exercise of this grace the test of fitness for heaven is that giving springs from love; the open hand is the result of the generous heart. Love, as someone has said, is the giving impulse, and where there is no giving there is no real love. And as heaven is the abode of love, no one is fit for the kingdom who has not the loving heart. But while it is true that there is no love where there is no giving, it is on the other hand true that you may have giving without love. That is the contingency the apostle contemplates here. He pictures a man bestowing all his goods to feed the poor. The Greek makes it plain that he doles his goods out to a large number of persons and that he doles them out with his own hand. He pictures a man doing the sort of thing Barnabas did when he sold his possessions and laid them at the apostles' feet. At first sight it seems to be magnificent, sacrificial giving. But even such giving as that may count for nothing and may profit a man nothing in the sight of God if it does not spring from real, genuine love. For as a mere matter of fact and experience, men give from all kinds of motives. They give sometimes because it is the correct thing to do, because it is good form to have their names on certain subscription lists. They give in order to stand well with their fellows and to win their applause. We have heard in this country of ours of men giving large sums to charities and philanthropies in the hope of winning for themselves titles and public honors. Strange and curious and sometimes sordid motives often prompt men to give. In their giving they are not thinking so much of the people who need help as of themselves. There were men of that type in our Lord's day. They gave their alms, He said, for to be seen of men. They got their reward in the shape of public applause. But there was nothing down to their credit in the account books of Almighty God. The motive that converts giving into a divine grace was lacking. Their giving sprang not from love, but from a perverted selfishness. And the apostle says much the same thing here. A man may give all his goods to the poor, but if he has not love, it profits him nothing in the sight of God. It is love that converts a gift into a grace. It is love that makes it a blessing to the recipient. You may give a dollar to a beggar in such a fashion as you might fling a bone to a dog—that while it ministers to his physical necessities it may wound his soul. On the other hand, you may give the smallest copper coin with such real sympathy that while it does not go far to minister to his bodily wants, it brings healing to his soul. You remember what Lowell says in his *Vision of Sir Launfal*:

> Not what we give, but what we share,—
> For the gift without the giver is bare;
> Who gives himself with his alms feeds three,—
> Himself, his hungering neighbor, and me.

But the special point the apostle makes here is that it is only love that makes a gift of value in the sight of God. The gift may relieve distress, but in God's sight it doesn't count. "It profiteth me nothing." Love is the alchemy that converts our humblest gifts and ministries into divine and heavenly graces. "Whosoever shall give to drink a cup of cold water only in the name of a disciple, he shall by no means lose his reward." It shall be set down to his credit in the great account books. But the critical words in that sentence are "in the

name of a disciple." Out of love for Jesus and those who name the
name of Jesus—that is what it means. It is the motive that determines
the value of a gift. Love makes every gift and every service precious
in the sight of God. But, if I bestow all my goods to feed the poor
and have not love—it profiteth me nothing.

And then the apostle takes the most extreme example of all. He
imagines a man sacrificing his life—and he says even that is nothing
without love. "Even though I give my body to be burned and have
not love, it profiteth me nothing." I do not know that without love
anybody would really give his body to be burned. It is quite true
that curious motives of pride, and eagerness for renown, and bravado,
played their part in the sufferings of the early Christian confessors.
But I do not suppose that anything but a supreme love for Christ
would have made them face the supreme trial of all. It was love that
made Ignatius face the lions in the amphitheater; it was love that
made the aged Polycarp endure the flames; it was love that made
children like Ponticus and Felicitas face death in its most terrible
forms. To such complete and absolute sacrifice only love is equal.
But the apostle takes the extremist illustration in order to enforce
his truth, and declares that if it is conceivable that a man should
give his body to be burned for any other motive than that of love it
would profit him nothing. But let love make him faithful unto death
and he would receive at God's hands the crown of life.

"Covet earnestly the best gifts," the apostle had said in the last
sentence of the preceding chapter. But here he speaks of a grace on
which the Corinthians had not reckoned, and yet without which
even the best gifts are worth nothing. Love is the one thing needful.
Without love, eloquence, prophecy, alms-giving, or courage do not
count. But with love, the stammering word, the trembling faith, the
widow's mite, the cup of cold water are of infinite value. All of
which amounts to this, that God tests deeds by motive. He does not
take them, shall I say, at their face value. The Lord trieth the heart.
Deeds are acceptable with Him as they are prompted and inspired
by right motives. "Is thine heart right?" That is God's question. And
the motive that gives value is love. Love is God's own character.
Love is the qualification for the kingdom. "Lovest thou Me?" is the
question that Jesus asks of men still, as He asked it of Peter of old.
Those who love share in the spirit of Jesus and belong to the kingdom
of love. But in that kingdom selfishness of any kind finds no place.
It is a truth calculated to make us search our hearts. We are still

inclined to worship gifts and shining endowments. But in God's sight character counts for more than gifts, and a loving heart is a better thing than the most dazzling endowments. Indeed, without love, if we had the eloquence of a Demosthenes, and the learning of a Bacon, and the lavish generosity of a Peabody, it would go all for nothing. All these things are just zeros until we put the digit of love in front of them. This very worship we are offering this morning, the gifts we have put upon those plates, the various kinds of service we try to render—they mean nothing without love. But if love prompts them, they become converted into things beyond price.

CHAPTER THREE

The Qualities of Love—Part 1

Love suffereth long and is kind; love envieth not; love vaunteth not itself, is not puffed up. —1 Corinthians 13:4

In the first three verses of this chapter—as we saw—Paul well-nigh exhausts language in setting forth the excellence of love. Indeed, in these first three verses Paul does more than assert the supremacy of love, he declares that it is love that gives every other gift its value. He names the very choicest gifts—tongues, prophecy, knowledge, faith, alms-giving, sacrificial courage—and declares that they amount to nothing without love. They are like a row of zeros with no numeral in front. And how much does a row of a dozen or a hundred, or a thousand zeros amount to? To nothing at all. There must be a digit in front to give zeros any value. And so it is love that gives every other gift its worth. A man might just as well not have these gifts as have them without love. They profit him nothing.

Well, after such an exordium as that we want to know what this love is like which the apostle rates so highly. How does he define it? As a matter of fact he doesn't define it. He tells us instead, how it works, how it reveals its presence. I question whether anyone could define love. The simplest and most elemental things always defy definition. What is music? Can you define it? You can say with the dictionary that it is "the science or art of tones." But would that give a man any idea of music—the thing that shakes and ravishes the soul? What is color? Can you define it? You can say with the dictionary again that it is "a property depending on the relations of light to the eye." But does that give a man any idea of color—the color of a sunset, for example—those glowing reds and purples that fill the soul with delight and subdue it into worship? What is a diamond? The chemist will tell you it is "native carbon in isometric crystals." He can tell you exactly how it is composed. But when he has given you his chemical formula, he has given you no idea of the diamond, that stone which seems to have imprisoned sunshine within itself, and which is able to flash it forth again in dazzling brilliance. Definitions do not carry us very far. There are some things that defy definition altogether. And love is one of these. The dictionary has to make an attempt at definition, so it describes love as "a feeling of strong attachment induced by that which delights or commands admiration." What a definition! You cannot fit the pattern love of all the love of God for men—into the four corners of that definition. God's love was not induced by something in us that delighted Him and commanded His admiration. "While we were yet sinners Christ died." You cannot fit in this dying of which Paul speaks in this chapter within the four corners of that definition. Look at the first thing he says about it: "Love suffereth long." He is thinking of wrongs and injuries inflicted by one man upon another and yet love holds on. It is not induced by something which delights. It persists in face of perversity and outrage. "A feeling of strong attachment induced by that which delights or commands admiration" may describe something that passes for love in our current speech, but it is wholly inadequate, absurdly inadequate to describe the αψαπν, the holy love of which Paul here speaks. I think the apostle himself felt that definition was impossible so instead of trying to define love he tells us in a series of sentences how love works, the kind of conduct in which love issues and through which it reveals itself.

Henry Drummond heads the chapter in which he discusses these verses, "The Analysis." Love is like light, he says. It is a compound thing. Just exactly as the scientist takes a beam of light and by passing it through a crystal prism, splits it up into its component colors—red and blue, yellow and violet, and all the colors of the rainbow—so Paul passes this thing love through the magnificent prism of his inspired intellect, and breaks it up into its elements, patience, kindness, generosity, humility and so on. Love, according to Drummond, is the sum of all these qualities.

For myself, I prefer to think of these things as the marks of love and the signs of love's presence. This is how you can tell that love is at work. Where love is, these things are also—they are the fruits of love. It is with love as it is with the spring. There are certain accompaniments of the spring, certain infallible signs of its presence. How do I know that spring has come? Not because the calendar tells me that on March 21 the winter is over and the spring has begun. March 21 may come and go without any sign of the arrival of the spring. How do I know that the spring has come? I know it because skies are blue and winds are balmy; I know it because everywhere about me I see signs of returning life; I know it because I catch sight of the yellow primrose and the dancing daffodils; I know it because of budding trees and bursting leaf; I know it because the birds again have broken out into song. These, and not a date in the calendar, are the real evidences of spring. It is when I see these sights and hear these sounds that I know that spring is here. And so it is with love. I suppose really that every one who professes to be a Christian ought to have this supreme gift of love. For the apostle says bluntly that he that loveth not knoweth not God. But alas! to have one's name on the church roll is no more proof of love than the date on the calendar is of the arrival of spring. There are certain things that go with love. There are certain ways in which it works. There are certain qualities which it always begets. It is when we see these qualities revealed in life and character that we can say with confidence, "Love is here."

Now the apostle has told us in the opening verses of this chapter that, without love, nothing is of any avail. Love is the one thing needful. Love is the wedding garment without which there is no place for us at the marriage feast of the King's Son. It is the court dress that gives the entree into the King's halls. "Above all these things," says the apostle in another place, "put on love, which is the bond of perfectness." This being so, and as life succeeds or fails according as we find ourselves in the King's palace or in the outer darkness at the finish, it is of vital importance that we should examine ourselves and see whether we really possess this supreme and indispensable grace of love. And we can always discover whether we possess it or not by turning the searchlight onto our lives and characters to see whether they bear the marks of love. "From henceforth let no man trouble me," said the apostle—having in mind some men who challenged and disputed his Christian standing, "for I bear branded on my body the marks of Jesus." The "marks of

Jesus" in Paul's case were the scars left on his face and head where the cruel stones had cut him, and the weals on his back where the strokes of the lash had fallen. He had borne these things out of devotion to his Lord. They were the brand of Jesus upon him. And these things which the apostle now proceeds to name are the marks of love, the signs of its presence. We can say we have love only as we possess these marks. And the first mark of love which the apostle mentions is this:

The Patience of Love

"Love suffereth long." Henry Drummond treats this as if it was equivalent to patience. But I am not sure that that is not to narrow unduly the meaning of the word. Dr. Thomas Charles Edwards, who has perhaps written the most massive commentary on this epistle, takes the view with some of the old church fathers, that it means greatness of soul, magnanimity. There is nothing petty or mean about love. It can rise clean above all petty, personal grievances. It can forget and ignore them. Love is too big and generous a thing to take account of them. But even if we translate the words, "love is magnanimous," it suggests a certain attitude towards injuries and wrongs. And in the New Testament the word has always a tacit reference to difficulties, sorrows, injuries, wrongdoing. So perhaps after all, we shall not be far wrong if we accept our English translation as setting forth the idea that was in Paul's mind: "love suffereth long." This is how love behaves in face of injuries and wrongs. It does not change to wrath and bitterness. It persists in loving. It doesn't break off relations: it holds on and loves on. It suffers long. The primal love of all, of which all other love is born, is the love of God. And love approaches perfection as it approximates to that primal love of God. And that is one of the characteristics of the love of God—it suffereth long. The Old Testament proclaims the truth. Across its pages I see written the words, "Love suffereth long." The Old Testament is practically the story of God's dealings with Israel. What infinite patience He showed! For Israel was constantly forgetting Him, rebelling against Him, breaking His covenant, betaking itself to the worship of false Gods. And yet God's love persisted and loved on. "How shall I give thee up, Ephraim?" "Can a woman forget her sucking child that she should not have compassion on the son of her womb? Yea, these may forget, yet will not I forget thee." He forgave and forgave and forgave this rebellious and wayward people. He did not cast them off. God's love suffered long. But it is in the New Testament, in the story of His Son Jesus that this quality in God's love shines out upon us in its wondrous and ineffable glory. In Jesus you see the love that suffereth long. Think of His dealings with those whom He called "friends." What blundering men those first disciples of His were! How they misunderstood Him! And how they must have grieved His heart. They conspired with the multitude to make Him an earthly King. James and John wanted to call down fire from heaven to destroy a Samaritan village! Peter took Him and rebuked Him because He dared even to hint at death! And yet Jesus bore with them. He did not wax impatient with them. Having loved His own He loved them even unto the end. His love survived even Peter's desertion and denial. "Go, tell His disciples and Peter," was the command given to the women on the first Easter morning. Love suffereth long. Think of His dealings with the people in general. He came unto His own and His own people received Him not. When Jesus discovered that rejection was going to be His lot—it would have been very human if He had shaken the dust of earth off His feet and had returned to the glory from which He had come—but so wonderful was His love for men that He loved on in spite of rejection and scorn, in spite of insult and hate, in spite of the buffeting and the spitting and the scourging; in spite of the Cross and the grave. He faced them all for love. He bore them all for love. The love of Christ suffered long.

Indeed, I need not go back to the New Testament to find proof and illustration that the love of Christ suffers long. We are ourselves the living evidences and monuments of it. For we are where we are on praying terms and with the hope of heaven in our souls—simply because the love of Christ suffers long. If He had been swift to mark iniquity, which of us should stand? If He had dealt with us after our sins or rewarded us according to our iniquities, where should we have been? For we have sinned and done wickedly. We have been perverse and wayward and rebellious. Every day and many a time in the day we do things that grieve Him. And yet He has not cast us off. He bears with us. When friends despair of us, His love pursues us still. It suffers long.

Indeed, Peter says that it is the long-suffering of the Lord which is our salvation. That really is a bit of autobiography. Peter was writing out of his own experience when he penned that sentence.

He had asked his Master one day, "Lord, how oft shall my brother sin against me and I forgive him? Until seven times?" And I have no doubt that when he suggested seven times, he thought he was making a most generous offer. But Jesus said to him, "I say not unto thee, until seven times, but until seventy times seven." Seventy times seven! Forgiveness without limit! And Peter came to need it all. He knew he was a saved man simply because of Christ's limitless forgiveness, the boundless patience of His love. And this is his confession, "The long-suffering of the Lord is salvation." And that is not Peter's confession only, it is our confession too, if we are serious men and women. Where should we have been if Christ only forgave until seven times? Amongst the castaways, in the outer darkness where there is weeping and wailing and gnashing of teeth. It is a day of mercy and grace with us still simply because our Lord's love suffers long. He forgives until seventy times seven. As our hymn expresses it, "Unwearied in forgiveness still, Thy heart could only love." The long-suffering of the Lord is salvation. And this is a mark of love in man as well as in God—it suffers long. It is infinitely patient even under wrongs and insults and injuries. We see that divine quality in the love parents have for wayward rebellious children. The younger son in the parable deeply wronged his father and well-nigh broke his heart. But the father's love held on, and when at last the wretched lad came home again there was no casting up of his wickedness in his teeth, there were no upbraidings or reproaches, but just a great outburst of loving welcome. "Bring forth the best robe and put it on him and put a ring on his hand and shoes on his feet, for this my son was dead and is alive again, and was lost and is found." My son! he said, of the lad who had wasted his substance: love suffereth long.

I heard recently a story about Dr. Lewis Edwards, a great Welsh divine of his day. He was preaching on one occasion in Festiniog about forgiveness, and urging the necessity of forgiving others if people themselves wished to be forgiven. And in his congregation there was a father and mother who had a wild scapegrace of a son, a lad who had given them no end of trouble and who even then was living a reckless sort of life in Liverpool. Dr. Edwards knew all about the trouble, and speaking to them after the service and making a personal application of his sermon, he said, "You must forgive John." "Forgive John," said the wife to the husband as they turned away, "he doesn't know our love for John." Forgive? Why, their hearts were with that absent lad, and that was what they prayed for with incessant entreaty, that he would come back. No! Dr. Edwards did not properly estimate a father's and mother's love. Many waters cannot quench love, neither can the floods drown it. Love suffereth long.

Well, let us search and try our hearts to see if we have love for this is one of the marks of love: it suffers long. We have all of us folk who have grieved us and offended us. What have we done with them? Broken off relations with them? Allowed love to change into contempt and dislike? But the very mark of love is that it is infinitely patient, it endures and persists, love suffereth long; and while all Christian people need this patient love, the Christian worker needs it in a special degree. Of course, he will not enter upon Christian work at all unless love inspires him, love for the Master and love for the people he seeks to serve. But if he is to do any good, his love must be a patient and enduring love. For there are all sorts of disappointments and failures to face. It is not a bit of use a man volunteering for the foreign mission field unless he has the love which suffers long—a love which persists in spite of the grossness and vileness of those amongst whom he labors, and the lapses and falls of those who have made profession of conversion. If a man gets angry and impatient when a convert goes astray, if he casts such a one off in despair—he had better stay at home. The mission field needs the love that suffers long. And so in only lesser degree does Christian work at home. The minister needs it, for results are slow in coming and men and women often sorely disappoint him. The teacher in the school needs it with a class of noisy boys or girls; if he gets impatient or loses his interest because the behavior of the children is trying and results disappointing, he is not going to be of very much use. In all our Christian work, in our attitude towards this world of sinning men and women, we need the love that suffers long. Have we got this love that reveals itself in the "patience which cannot know defeat" and the "pity which will not be denied"?

The Beneficence of Love

And the second mark of love is this—it is "kind." These two first marks of love are like the opposite sides of the same coin. The one is the passive and the other the active aspect of love. "Long suffering," as Dr. Edwards puts it, expresses the self-restraint of Christian love; kindness expresses its self-abandonment. Love not only bears patiently wrongs and injuries, but it gives itself away in beneficent and unselfish service. Love is not merely passive—it is positive and energetic. It is kind. It "does kindnesses." It is actively beneficent. Once again, to see what is meant by this mark of love, suppose we turn to the life of our Lord. There was all the passive patience and endurance of love in His life. In spite of hate and rejection, suffering and death, His love held on. But it was not a case simply of holding on with Jesus. His love constrained Him to a life of ceaseless beneficence. He went about doing good. Jesus was kind in that sense. He did kindnesses. He was always doing them. He never did anything else. Think of Him at the marriage feast at Cana. That wine should run short on such an occasion would have covered the bridegroom with shame. And so, to prevent any shadow falling upon the feast, Jesus turned the water into wine. It was the sheer kindness of love. Or think of that other day when He was again approaching Cana and just outside the gates He met a little funeral—the funeral of an only son. Unasked, Jesus stopped the procession and bade the dead man arise. "And He gave him to his mother." It was love expressing itself in sheer kindness. Or think of Him in that desert place with that crowd of over five thousand hanging upon His lips. And lest out of sheer weariness any of them should faint by the way, He Himself out there in the wilderness provided them with a full table. It was the love of His soul revealing itself in kindness. Or think of Him in that last dread scene when He hung upon the cross in mortal pain, forgetting all about His own agony that He might comfort the dying robber who had cried to Him in a penitence that was well-nigh despair. "Today," said He, "thou shalt be with Me in Paradise." Love in the case of Jesus not only suffered long, but it was kind. It was not only infinitely patient, it was actively beneficent. Love is always kind. And by being kind I mean, and the apostle means, not simply that love makes a person genial in temper, but it constrains him to do good. After all, a genial and kindly temper is quite consistent with a selfish neglect of the need and woe of the world. I dare say Dives was genial enough, but he did nothing to help Lazarus. A man may be a good fellow without doing a hand's turn to bless the world. But love, this holy love of which the apostle here speaks, does kindnesses. The root of the Greek verb which Paul uses here is a word which means "useful." Love is useful. It is practically helpful. It does things. It imparts benefits. It does kindnesses. There can be no love where there is no active kindness. You can no more have love without kindness than you can have a springtime without flowers. And just as inevitably as the spring brings the flowers, so does love issue in the kind deed. And there is so much need for kindness. The world is full of pain and sorrow and loneliness and grief. And it is so easy to be kind. For kindness does not need money. Kindness may be expressed in money sometimes, but it can be expressed just as surely in a word. A word of comfort or cheer, a clasp of the hand, a visit, an invitation to the home—how easily these things can be given or done. And what measureless good they may do! And what an infinite reward they bring! Henry Drummond quotes this sentence: "The greatest thing a man can do for His Heavenly Father is to be kind to some of His other children." And, unless I read my New Testament altogether amiss, it is by the test of kindness that our fitness for heaven will be discovered. For the people who are invited to inherit the kingdom are the people who visited the sick and clothed the naked, and fed the hungry and gave water to the thirsty—in a word, the people who did kindnesses; while the people who failed to visit the sick and help the poor and clothe the naked, in a word, the people who were not kind, are bidden depart into the everlasting fire. And the reason for that is this: heaven is the abode of love, and where there is no kindness there is no love. Have we this mark of kindness? That is a beautiful story which is told about the late Sir Bartle Frere. A gentleman who was to be his host, but who had never met him, wanted to know how he should identify him. The answer was this: "If you see a tall gentleman helping somebody—that will be Sir Bartle Frere." What a beautiful description! But ought not that to be the description of every Christian? If love is in our hearts, shall we not always be helping somebody? for love is kind. Let us pray that this mark of kindness may be upon us all. It is the convincing evidence of love. Henry Drummond concludes his paragraph on kindness with an old and familiar quotation. I might just as well finish this sermon with it too.

"I shall pass through this world but once. Any good thing therefore that I can do, or any kindness that I can show to any human being, let me do it now. Let me not defer it, or neglect it, for I shall not pass this way again."

Chapter Four

The Qualities of Love—Part 2

Love envieth not, love vaunteth not itself, is not
puffed up.   *—1 Corinthians 13:4*

In the opening sermon in this brief series of expositions of Paul's great hymn in praise of love, I called attention to the fact that the practical problem which was confronting the apostle at this point was the problem of the divisions and factions and jealousies which prevailed in the church at Corinth. Even in this chapter in which the thought of the glory of love in itself seems to absorb and possess his soul, the distracted condition of the church at Corinth is never out of his mind. It is love as the cure for strife, love as the one sure way to unity that he is thinking of all the time. And all that reveals itself with special clearness in those qualities of love which are to engage our attention this morning. What was the real root from which the divisions in the church at Corinth sprang? They sprang from jealousy and envy. The man who spoke with tongues was jealous of the man who prophesied; the man who prophesied was jealous of the man who spoke with tongues. There was only one effectual cure for that condition of things and that was love. As the apostle says, love envieth not, love vaunteth not itself, is not puffed up. Once the envy was vanished, the longed-for unity would return.

Love and Envy
"Love envieth not"! The apostle could not have said a more

wonderful thing about love than that. For envy, according to the old Book, was the direct cause of the first crime in the story of the race, and envy is the last vice to be eradicated out of the breast of the regenerated saint. "Of all other affections," says Bacon, "envy is the most importune and continual. For of other affections there is occasion given but now and then, but envy never takes a holiday, for it is ever working upon some or other. It is also the vilest affection and the most depraved: for which cause it is the proper attribute of the Devil, who is called 'The Envious Man that soweth tares amongst the wheat by night.'" That is a terrible description which the great Moralist gives of envy—the most "depraved and vile of the affections and the most importune and continual." But terrible though the description is, we know it is only too terribly true. Envy is the most importune and continual of all the affections. It affects us all. Its baleful fires scorch us every day. Every day we feel its pangs and torments. Envy is borne of the inequalities between men—inequalities of gift, inequalities of position, inequalities of attainment. I am not concerned at the moment to explain these inequalities. I don't know that they ever can be explained. We can only say that so it has been decreed by the sovereign will of Almighty God. It is quite possible that some of these inequalities may be modified—the inequalities of condition, for example. But there are other and deeper and more significant inequalities that nothing we can do can ever affect. I mean inequalities of mental endowment, and moral vigor, and even physical strength. These inequalities have always been in our world and apparently they will remain to the world's end; from these inequalities envy springs. There were inequalities between the two first men born upon this earth, and the inequalities begot raging, deadly, murderous envy. This is how the old Book tells the story: "And Abel was a keeper of sheep, but Cain was a tiller of the ground. And in process of time it came to pass that Cain brought of the fruit of the ground an offering unto the Lord. And Abel, he also brought of the firstlings of his flock and of the fat thereof. And the Lord had respect unto Abel and unto his offering. But unto Cain and to his offering he had not respect. And Cain was very wroth and his countenance fell. And the Lord said unto Cain, Why art thou wroth? and why is thy countenance fallen? If thou doest well, shalt thou not be excepted? and if thou doest not well sin coucheth at the door." Strip the old story of its old-world setting and get to the heart of it and it means this: Cain envied his brother because of his superior goodness and consequent favor with God. Cain was on fire with murderous hate of his own flesh and blood because he couldn't bear to think that Abel was better than he. Even the solemn warning of God Himself did not avail to quench that devastating flame, and the end of the story is this: "And it came to pass when they were in the field that Cain rose up against Abel his brother and slew him." And Cain lives on in every heart. "Let the holy man here who has never had this same hellfire in his heart at his brother," says Dr. Alexander Whyte in a grimly searching passage, "at his dearest and best and only friend on earth, at his old playfellow, at his present fellow-worshipper, let that happy man cast stones at that miserable wretch with murder in his heart at Abel his unsuspecting brother." Well, if only those who had never known the pangs of envy were allowed to fling a stone at Cain, how many stones would be flung? It is the most importune of all the affections. It attacks us all. As Shakespeare puts it in his *Troilus and Cressida:*

> The general's disdained
> By him one step below: he, by the next;
> That next by him beneath; so every step,
> Exampled by the first pace that is sick
> Of his superior, grows to an envious fever
> Of pale and bloodless emulation.

We are all of us envious of the man who is above ourselves. "Near kinsfolk and fellows in office and those that have been bred together," says Bacon again, "are more apt to envy their equals when they are raised." So devilish an affection is envy that we cannot hear of the advancement even of a friend without some sort of pang. We are all of us guilty in this matter. Have you, man of business, never envied the man who has proved more successful than yourself? Have you, woman, never envied your sister who is more brilliant and who occupies a higher place in society than you do? Have you, preacher, never felt the pangs of envy when you heard another preacher praised for his eloquence, or his pastoral fidelity, or his personal piety? Alas! yes, we have all to plead guilty. This most vile and depraved of the affections has found a place in our hearts again and again and again.

And just as envy filled the church at Corinth with division and strife, so it is the principal root of the bitterness that fills our world

today. We are all jealous of the man who is just above us and envious
of his lot. And the envy begets hate, and the hate issues in strife and
we bite and devour one another. Now let no one charge me with
wishing to maintain the status quo or preaching a doctrine of laissez-
faire or suggesting that as things are so they must remain. There are
injustices whose continuance we ought not to tolerate for a single
moment. There are giant wrongs which we ought to strain every
power to remove. There are conditions of life which never give the
children born into them any sort of a chance. We cannot and dare not
sit down and fold our hands in face of these things. But when we
have redressed injustices and banished wrongs and created decent
conditions, differences will still remain. Some men will be abler and
stronger and more gifted than others; some will be masters and some
will be servants; some will be captains of industry and some will be
privates in the ranks; differences will give occasion for envy, and
envy will still lead on to strife. There is one real hope for unity and
peace in our broken and disordered world, as there was only one real
hope of unity in the quarrelsome church at Corinth, and that is in the
spread of this spirit of holy love—for love envieth not. Real love, far
from begrudging the success of another, rejoices in it. If you want to
see the working of the love which envieth not, read the story of the
relations between John the Baptist and Jesus. John was the most
conspicuous preacher in Palestine until Jesus came. But when Jesus
began to preach, John fell back into the second place. But some of his
disciples felt jealous of Jesus and they tried to kindle some sort of
envy in the heart of John. "Rabbi," they said to him, "He that was
with thee beyond Jordan, to whom thou hast borne witness, behold
the same baptizeth and all men come to Him." But John had the love
which envieth not. "He that hath the bride," he said, "is the bridegroom,
but the friend of the bridegroom which standeth and heareth him,
rejoiceth greatly because of the bridegroom's voice: this my joy
therefore is fulfilled. He must increase, but I must decrease." Or read
of the relations between Barnabas and Saul. When Barnabas found
the work at Antioch becoming too much for him single-handed, he
began to look round for someone whom he could invite to share his
labors. And his mind reverted to Saul, the converted rabbi, who was
living in something like seclusion in Tarsus. Now if Barnabas had
had a scrap of jealousy in his soul he would never have chosen Saul
for a colleague. For Saul was an abler man than himself. Saul was
bound inevitably by sheer ability to take first place. But Barnabas had

a heart too big for mean and ugly considerations of place and position. All he cared for was his Lord and the work and the souls of men. He had the love which envieth not, and so he went forth to Tarsus to seek for Saul, and when he had found him he brought him to Antioch.

Love envieth not! And the reason for that is at any rate twofold. This first, that so far as earthly gains and prizes are concerned (which are the most frequent cause of envy), love envieth not because it has another and quite different scale of values. The love of which Paul speaks in this chapter does not set its heart on houses and lands and this world's wealth and fame. Its heart is set on God and things eternal. It is intent not on getting goods, but on being good. Like the pilgrims in Vanity Fair, it lifts its eyes from the glittering prizes of earth and has its trade and traffic in heaven and buys only the truth. It counts all things but loss if it may gain Christ. Worldly success never stirs a pang of envy in love's heart, it has another and nobler scale of value.

And a second reason is this—love delights not to get but to give. Love, as someone has defined it, is the giving impulse. So that far from grudging the good things that come to another, it rejoices in them. Envy, on the other hand, is essentially selfish. Self fills the envious man's vision. He is always comparing other men with himself and grudges to others anything that seems to lift them above himself. Love is the exact antithesis of all that. In real love there can be no shred of envy, for in its nature it is unselfish and sacrificial. We can see love without a trace of envy in the love of parents for their children. It happens very often that children attain a measure of success their parents never reached. But there is no bitter pang of envy when news of a son's achievements reaches the old home— nothing but thankfulness and rejoicing. I knew a minister of ours whose son had reached one of the highest places in our English life. The father's delight in his son's triumphs was beautiful to behold. His eye glistened and his face shone as he spoke of him. The son's success caused no pang of jealousy to the older man. Love envieth not, and to the father's loving heart the son's fame was a source of purest gladness. And as love for our brothers takes possession of our souls this ugly and bitter affection will disappear from our souls. For love always thinks of another's needs before its own, and rejoices over another's gladness more than its own. Love, because of its nature, envieth not.

Paul knew that if only this love were shed abroad in the hearts of the Corinthian Christians envy would die, and they would thank God for one another's gifts, and a happy and concordant church would be the result; and if only this love were shed abroad in human hearts, this love that seeks to give rather than to get, this unselfish sacrificial love—envy would die, and with the passing of envy, strife and friction would pass as well. There would still be differences, but the world would be a peaceful, happy and cooperant world, for the differences would beget no bitterness inasmuch as each would serve one another in love. The cure for the world's woe is to be sought in the love which envieth not.

Love And Pride

"Love," the apostle adds, "vaunteth not itself, is not puffed up." These two qualities of love are closely related to each other. "Is not puffed up" refers to inward disposition; "vaunteth not itself" refers to outward conduct and behavior. It is because men are puffed up that they vaunt themselves. It is because they have an exaggerated sense of their own importance that they strut and swagger before their associates. The apostle here again is thinking of the Corinthian church and its disputations and quarrelsome members. Each was puffed up with a sense of the importance of his gift, and vaunted himself over his neighbor who had another and different kind of gift. The man who had the gift of tongues especially, thought there was no gift to compare to it, and so he boasted himself over the man who had the plainer and more practical gift of prophecy. And the self-importance and the boasting led to friction and strife. And the cure for that, according to the apostle, is love, for love vaunteth not itself, is not puffed up. There is no brag or swank or swagger about love. The mark of love is a beautiful modesty and humility. And why is it love vaunteth not itself, is not puffed up? Mr. Percy Ainsworth suggests that the "inner truth about the humility of love is to be found in its greatness." The big things never vaunt themselves. They do not swagger. They do not need to. It is always the smaller things that strut and insist upon their self-importance. It was the frog in Aesop's fable that tried to blow itself up into the size of a cow. It is the man who is not quite sure of his position in society who stands on his dignity. The really big man has no need. The man who is a third cousin to a duke never allows you to forget it. The duke himself makes no fuss about it. I have known some preachers touchy and self-important enough—a great man like John

Clifford had no need to insist upon himself. We speak of empty boasting. There is no other kind of boasting, says Mr. Percy Ainsworth. The very nature and essence of the boast is emptiness. The modern psychologists are fond of saying that vehemence of assertion is often only a cloak for inward uncertainty and doubt. And so all boasting and self-inflation are evidence and advertisement of poverty. The big things don't boast. The sun does not boast. The mountains do not boast. The great and wide sea does not boast. They do not need to puff themselves up. Their greatness is plain, obvious, unmistakable. And love has no need to vaunt itself or puff itself up. It is the greatest thing in the world, and its greatness cannot be denied. It is like the sun, the mountain, the sea—great beyond challenge or dispute.

Now all that, I have no doubt, is entirely true, but I do not think it touches the real point. Why does a man puff himself up and vaunt himself? To demonstrate his own greatness, and especially to prove his superiority to his neighbor. The man who spoke with tongues tried in this way to establish his superiority to the man who had only the more commonplace and pedestrian gift of prophecy. But love never seeks to assert its superiority, love ever seeks to serve. The man in whose heart love burns never seeks to be first, he aspires rather to be the servant of all. A certain gracious and beautiful humility is of the very nature of love. Recall, for example, some of the characteristics of Him who was love incarnate. He did great deeds of mercy. But He never advertised Himself. He did not strut or cry or lift up His voice in the streets. When He had healed the leper He gave him instructions to tell no man. Jesus did not parade His goodness. He did not vaunt Himself. He was satisfied just to serve the sick and the afflicted. "He would that no man should know it." There are some who will not take part in any philanthropic movement unless they are given the first place, unless their names are trumpeted abroad. But that is not the temper of love. Love is modest. Love is ready to stoop. Love cares nothing for its own reputation so long as it can serve. Think again of Jesus on that dark betrayal night. On their way to the Upper Room the disciples had been disputing as to who of them was greatest. Each of them had been emphasizing his own claims to the highest place. And the result was that when they came to the Upper Room and took their seats, no one would stoop to the humble but grateful task of foot-washing. None of them would act as servant to the rest. So Jesus

Himself riseth from supper and laying aside His garments, He took a towel and girded Himself; then He poureth water into the basin and began to wash the disciples' feet and to wipe them with the towel wherewith He was girded. And in that deed of our Lord's we see love in action. He, the Greatest, stooped to the lowliest service. And thereby He revealed the true nature of love. For love never vaunts itself, or puffs itself. Love does not seek to be superior, love only seeks to serve.

And perhaps there is one other reason, too, why love vaunts not itself and is not puffed up. The love of which Paul here speaks looks up to God as well as looks out to man. And the love that has once looked up to God knows that it has nothing to boast itself of. The love which is begotten of God knows that there is nothing to justify one swelling thought of pride. "We love," says St. John, "because He first loved us." And He loved us not because we deserved it. He loved us in spite of our ill deserts. "While we were yet sinners Christ died." And He continues to love us still in spite of folly, and perversity, and sin. It is free, unmerited, undeserved love—the love which God bestows upon us. And the love we give is but a poor and unworthy return. Love is never in any mood to boast. It vaunteth not itself, is not puffed up. For it knows that its own acceptance is all of grace. Humility and modesty is the very mark of love. It never brags of its gifts and services. It knows that the best it can do is not to be mentioned alongside that mighty love which for our sakes bore the Cross. Envy and pride—these are the two most prolific causes of the world's misery and woe. Love, real love, would banish them both. And love is the mark of the Christian. Do we bear this mark? "Love envieth not, love vaunteth not itself, is not puffed up." Are we free from envy, free from pride? How love of this kind would sweeten the world! Envy—that is the feeling that the lesser cherishes towards the greater. Pride—that is the attitude the greater assumes towards the lesser! Perhaps if there were no pride on the one side, there would not be so much envy on the other! It is superciliousness and the swagger of superiority that irritates and angers. Perhaps if those of us that are better off had the love that vaunteth not itself, is not puffed up—those less well off would have the love that envieth not. I read a beautiful little story about Principal Cairns the other day. He was one of Scotland's greatest men. He had the offer of the principalship of Edinburgh University, but he preferred to serve his church as principal of the theological college. Modesty was the supreme characteristic of this great man's nature. On public occasions he was accustomed to stand back and let others pass him, saying: "You first, I follow." It became the habit of his life, this love which never vaunted itself. When he was dying he said farewell to those he loved, but his lips continued still to move. They bent to catch the final word, which doubtless was spoken to Him who was dearer than life: "You first, I follow." And if we all had that spirit, if in honor we preferred one another and served each other in love, we should get rid of envy too, and love triumphant would make earth like heaven.

CHAPTER FIVE

The Qualities of Love—Part 3

Doth not behave itself unseemly, seeketh not its own.
—1 Corinthians 13:5

Dr. Thomas Charles Edwards, commenting on this verse, thinks that in this further description of love as something which does not "behave itself unseemly," the apostle has still the condition of the church at Corinth in his mind. For the rivalry and jealousy that prevailed amongst the members of the church led directly to unseemly behavior in the conduct of public worship. To understand how this could be, we must remember that worship in the early church was a much more free and spontaneous thing than it is with us. There were not set or stereotyped orders of service such as we have in our churches today. Worship was not standardized. It did not follow any fixed plan. We place the conduct of worship in the hands of persons specially set apart to that work. But in the Corinthian church there was no person corresponding to what we call the "stated minister." When the Christians gathered together for worship no one knew who was going to take part in it—for the simple reason that it was open to anyone to take part if he was moved to it by the Holy Spirit. I suppose theoretically the Friends' meeting reproduces the practice of the early church as nearly as anything we have today—for the theory of the Friends' worship is that anyone moved by the Spirit may participate. But in actual experience the modern Friends' meeting is very unlike the meetings of the Corinthian church.

For while the characteristic feature of the Friends' meetings is a reverential silence and devoutness, the characteristic of the meetings of this Corinthian church was noise and confusion and disorder. This was due in part to the wealth of spiritual gifts the Corinthians enjoyed. When the Spirit of God comes in full flood upon a community it cannot be confined within fixed and rigid forms. During the Welsh Revival orders of service were flung aside for a whole twelve-month: the minister became almost a superfluity because all kinds of people wanted to take part in the worship. It was like that in Corinth. Paul tells us all about it in the next chapter. When the people came together each one had a psalm, or a teaching, or a revelation, or a tongue, or an interpretation which they wished to contribute. So eager were they to do this that they brought the worship into disorder, and gave rise to scenes calculated to bring the blush of shame to the cheek of anyone really concerned for the good name of Christ's church. For what happened was this, that people who were endowed with the gift of tongues insisted upon speaking all at once, so that in the next chapter the apostle lays down the rule that not more than two or three should speak with tongues at one service, and that they should speak in turn; and they were not to speak at all if there were not an interpreter present who could make what they said intelligible to the congregation. And the prophets apparently were not very much better than the men who had the gift of tongues, for every man was so convinced that what he had to say was so important that he insisted on saying it even though another prophet was addressing the church at the time. So Paul speaks sharply to the prophets. They must not plead that the impulse of the Spirit was irresistible. "The spirits of the prophets," he says, "are subject to the prophets." And he lays down the rule that the prophets are to prophesy one by one, so that all may learn and all may be comforted. God is not a God of confusion, he says, but of peace. And he finishes up his discussion of the public worship of the church with the exhortation, "Let all things be done decently, and in order."

He has all these disorderly conditions of worship in his mind when he pens this sentence, "Love doth not behave itself unseemly." Unseemly behavior would be forever banished from the church if the Christians learned really to love one another. For what did the disorder and confusion arise from? Was it not from this—that every man considered his own contribution more important than everyone else's? that each was intent on his own glory? At the root of all this unseemliness there lay self-importance, pride, and self-conceit. But love could never be guilty of any such unseemliness, for the simple but sufficient reason that love seeketh not its own. In my text I believe the second clause gives the reason for the first. Love seeketh not its own—love could make every man think his neighbor better than himself. Love would make men willing to give place to one another. Love would always say, "You first, I follow." And so the vulgar competition that made a veritable Babel of public worship would cease. Love doth not behave itself unseemly, because it seeketh not its own.

Now I believe that Dr. Thomas Charles Edwards is right in thinking that the apostle had an eye to church worship when he penned this passage. But the sentence must not be limited in its application to church worship. It admits, as Dr. Edwards himself says, of a much wider application than that. It is a little sentence which describes the very nature of love, and not simply how love acts in a certain contingency. A certain seemliness of behavior is of the very essence of love. This is true, for example, of all real love between man and woman. There is always an element of reverence and almost of worship about true love. Love never degrades the object of its love by behaving unseemly towards it. A man who truly loves can be trusted anywhere with the woman of his affection. She will be sacred in his eyes. Neither by deed nor word will he do anything to stain or sully her purity. He will pay her high and chivalrous honor and respect. "Love doth not behave itself unseemly." This needs to be said in these days, for this word *love* is far too freely used. It has been bandied about in the law courts in connection with cases which have shocked and scandalized every decent man and woman. They have used the word of people who were false to one another and who flung chastity and honor to the winds. But love is not the word to use about the relations of those men and women who have been standing in the pillory of public shame. The right word to use is not love but *lust*—ugly, vulgar, vile lust. For love doth not behave itself unseemly.

It needs to be said also to the fiction writers of our day. They picture love for us as wallowing in the gutter and reveling in filth. Mr. Nevinsohn the other day declared that the way to make money was to play with the indecent. He instanced a book which had reached a very large sale on the strength of a sensual and suggestive chapter with which it ended. He himself had been doomed to poverty because he had refused to dip his pen in filth. Well, Mr. Nevinsohn need not envy those who line their pockets by smudging the minds of their readers. They shall bear their judgment whosoever they be. But it is about time to protest against the word *love* being prostituted to these base uses. Love and indecency, love and filth have nothing to say to one another. They are poles apart. Let these purveyors of sensuality call a spade a spade, and give this foul thing of which they write its proper name of lust. But let them take their foul hands off love, for love is a holy, austere, and sacred thing. Love never cheapens or degrades the loved one. Love is chivalrous, reverential, worshipful. Love doth not behave itself unseemly. Let youth remember that! They are sinning against love, proving that what they have is not love at all, if they indulge in word or deed that offends against propriety and honor. For that is the mark of love, it doth not behave itself unseemly.

But it is not simply or even chiefly of the love of man for woman that the apostle is thinking of here, but of love in its very broadest sense as the feeling we ought to cherish towards all men. And what he says here is that if we have such love in our hearts it will preserve us from all ugly and unseemly behavior, for love, to quote Dr. Moffatt's translation, "is never rude."

Love and Behavior

This is love in society, Henry Drummond says, love in relation to etiquette. Paul extols love in this sentence as the most effective teacher of politeness and high courtesy. I have seen exposed for sale in shop windows books that are called "manuals of etiquette." I have never examined any one of them, but I suppose they are occupied with what are supposed to be the manners and customs of good society. They tell the reader what is supposed to be good form: how to dress on special occasions, how to pay calls, how to behave at table, and so on, and so on. Well, I dare say these manuals serve a useful purpose. They may help to set a man at ease in a society to which he has not been accustomed, though I can quite imagine that they may also have the effect of making a man's manners stiff, and constrained and artificial. But better than all your manuals of etiquette is love. Love can never be rude. Love begets courtesy, and gentleness and consideration, and those are the gifts that make the fine-mannered lady or gentleman. Drummond quotes

Carlyle's saying about Robert Burns, that there was no truer gentleman in Europe than the ploughman-poet. And he accounts for it by saying that Burns loved everything—the mouse and the daisy and all the things great and small, that God had made. "So, with this simple passport," he says, "he could mingle with any society and enter courts and palaces from his little cottage on the banks of the Ayr." I do not know that the illustration is the most happily chosen, but the point Drummond is making is absolutely right. Set a man with a loving heart in the midst of any society and he will be at his ease in it. For he will possess that fine courtesy which is the hallmark of the true gentleman. For courtesy, after all, is not to be taught by rule. It is an emanation of the spirit. No selfish man can be really courteous. He may have a certain surface polish that enables him to pass muster in society. But chivalry and courtesy can never grow in a selfish heart. They are the offspring of love. Unselfish thought for others lies at the very heart of them. It is love alone that makes the gentleman—for love is never rude, love doth not behave itself unseemly.

Mr. Percy Ainsworth, in his very suggestive chapter on this phrase, says that one might think for a moment that the apostle in these words is handling his great theme with a lighter and more superficial touch. "Seemliness suggests the ideas of tact and delicacy, judgment and propriety. It stands in the minds of many not so much for right itself as for a way of being right and doing right. It relates to shape rather than to substance, to manner rather than to essence. It is the pattern and not the fabric." Within limits, that is true. Seemly behavior is not so much a description of love itself as of the kind of conduct in which it issues. It is one of the accompaniments and consequences of love rather than one of its essential notes. And yet that distinction may easily be pressed too far. And in any case, because it deals with external conduct, seemly behavior is not to be dismissed as a subsidiary and unimportant thing. Of course there is a seemly behavior which is perilous. It is that which, as Mr. Ainsworth says, "is secured by a tactful but immoral acceptance of things as you find them." It is the sort of seemliness suggested by the old proverb, Do in Rome as the Romans do. That kind of seemliness is the refuge of the timid and the cowardly and is a cloak for half the sin of the world. But that is not the seemliness of which the apostle is thinking. I said in my opening sermon that love, as the apostle thinks of it, looks up to God, and then looks out to man. The idea of right and truth is central to it. It is not the seemly that is right in love's eyes, but the thing that is right is also the thing that is seemly. Love is as loyal to the right as the needle is to the Pole.

But while inflexibly loyal to the right, love seeks to do the right in love's own seemly way. To do the right is good, but to do the right in a fine way is still better. And that is exactly what love teaches us to do. Love is not only right and true, but it is delicate and tactful and courteous. Love is never boorish and rough. It is amazing how many good people take all the grace off their good deeds by the way in which they do them. They give alms, for example. They help a man who is down, but along with the money they give so much advice, and indulge in so much scolding, that the recipient is hurt and bruised and but for his desperate need would like to fling his gift back at them. Or they take upon themselves to warn a man against a certain fault. The fault may be real, and the warning may have been urgently necessary, but they do it so roughly, mistaking brutal directness for honesty, that instead of helping the man concerned and bringing him to repentance, they make him angry and harden him in his sin. Again and again we take all the grace off actions in themselves good by the way in which we do them: "We practice one virtue at the expense of another." We pride ourselves on our honesty and neglect sympathy. We make a boast of our candor and forget to be kind. One can understand why the little girl prayed, "O God, make all the bad people good," and then added, "and make all the good people nice."

Paul made exactly the same distinction when he said that scarcely for a righteous man would one die, but for a good man one would even dare to die. The righteous man is the man who is merely good and just, the good man is nice into the bargain. And love, when it takes possession of the heart, makes a man's goodness nice. It makes him do his fine things in a fine way. It makes a gentleman of him. For what is a gentleman after all but a man of gentle spirit and kindly deeds? And love alone can make a man that. We have an old saying to the effect that manners maketh man. I am not quite sure of that, but I am quite sure that the manners are an index to the man. A man expresses himself in his manners. And if the man has love in his heart, it will show itself in kindness and courtesy. For love is never rude, doth not behave itself unseemly. Well, what about this mark? Do we possess it? I am not asking whether we are masters of the conventions and usage of society. I am asking whether we have the loving spirit that teaches us an instructive courtesy? Or do we go through life jostling, battering and bruising people by our brusqueness and rudeness? At any rate let us take to heart this truth—it is love that marks the Christian and love makes a man chivalrous and courteous and fine mannered, for love is never rude, doth not behave itself unseemly.

Love and Unselfishness

And now, in considering the next phrase, "love seeketh not its own," I want to begin by repeating what I said above, that in this phrase we have the secret and explanation of the former. Unseemly behavior is nearly always the result of pushfulness and selfishness. But love never behaves itself unseemly for the simple reason that it seeketh not its own. To revert for a moment to that unseemliness in the conduct of worship about which Paul has so much to say in the next chapter, it all arose because all the people who had spiritual gifts insisted upon being heard and no one would give way to anyone else. At the root of it all there lay a very ugly self-conceit. But the mark of love is that it never seeks its own. It always willingly makes way for others. If only there had been some of this unselfish love in the hearts of the Corinthian Christians there would have been no disorder in worship. Love doth not behave itself unseemly, because it seeketh not its own.

And, speaking in the general sense, it can be truly said that unselfishness is the secret of high courtesy to this day. Fine manners, true gentlemanliness are not a matter of rich clothing or titles, or surface politeness, they are born of the unselfish spirit. A man may have rich clothes and titles, and polished manners, and yet events may show him to be no real gentleman. Somehow just at this point the memory of that terrible fire which took place at a charity bazaar in Paris long years ago comes back to my mind. The place was filled with titled folk, the very elite of Paris society. When the fire broke out there was a mad rush for the door. Those rich and titled folk fought and struggled with one another to get out of the fiery inferno. Nobody paid attention to consideration of age or sex— every one was for himself and the devil might take the hindmost. The gentleman that day was not to be found amongst those so-called leaders of society intent only on saving their own skins, but in that humble paper-seller who, taking his own life in his hands, ventured into the blazing building again and again to rescue those who would otherwise have been burned to death. The selfish and self-seeking mob made a poor showing on that day of testing. But the love that did not seek its own, did not behave itself unseemly even in that fiery trial. It is the unselfish spirit that makes the gentleman. If we are intent upon our own place and position, we are sure to be rough and pushful, we are sure to bruise and hurt some people as we make our way through life. But if we have the love which seeketh not its own, then in life's sharpest crises we shall not behave ourselves unseemly.

Moreover not only is this quality in love the source and spring of all chivalrous courtesy, but this phrase brings us to love's essence. Love seeketh not its own. Love lives not to get but to give. All love is of God, the apostle says. The love of God is the original primal love of which our human love is born. Just as all the various forms of light that we enjoy have been kindled at the central fires of the sun, so every one that loveth is born of God. God's love is the original love, and if we want to know what love is like, we must see it in God. Well, I consider the love of God—and this is the kind of love I see—a love that seeketh not its own. God has been seeking man, giving Himself to man from the beginning of time. God is love, and just because He is love He could not live in the enjoyment of a selfish glory. God seeks not His own glory, but our good. When man went astray God did not cast him adrift and cut off all communication between this world and His heaven. He went after this sinning, perverse, and rebellious child of His. He sacrificed Himself in order to find and save him. "God so loved the world that he gave His only begotten Son." And when we turn our gaze from the Father to the Son, it is the same quality of love that we see—a love that never sought its own, a love that gave.itself and squandered itself and sacrificed itself to the uttermost. Love seeketh not its own. From start to finish Jesus' life is an illustration and example of unselfish love. You might write that sentence over the manger at Bethlehem, "Love seeketh not its own," for it was to save us—the Eternal Son took flesh, and in order to do that He had to empty Himself. You might write it across the story of His earthly ministry, "Love seeketh not its own," for He bore our griefs and carried our sorrows: He lived not to be ministered unto but to minister. He sought not His own ease or comfort. He sought only to help and heal, and you might write this word upon the cross on which He died, "Love seeketh not its own." "He saved others," said the mocking spectators, "Himself He cannot save." And they spoke better than they knew. He couldn't save Himself because He was intent on saving others. It was not the ropes and nails that kept Him hanging on that cross. There were not nails and ropes enough in Jerusalem to keep Him there had He wished to come down. He could have summoned legions of angels to His help if He had wished to escape out of the hands of His foes. But His love kept Him there—that mighty love that never sought its own. It was not His own comfort or glory that Jesus sought, but the souls of men. He sought to save them from the bondage and guilt and penalty of sin. And since He could do it in no other or cheaper way, He bore our sins in His body on to the tree:

> He died that we might be forgiven,
> He died to make us good,
> That we might go at last to heaven,
> Saved by His precious blood.

The Cross is just the supreme example of the love that seeketh not its own. This is an infallible mark of love—unselfishness. Does it characterize our lives? What are we living for? For ourselves? For our own pleasure? For our own enrichment? For our own success? For our own fame? Is that it? Turn the searchlight of a phrase like this on to your own lives—"love seeketh not its own" and how do you come out of the test? Is self at the center? That is not love's way. Love gives and spends and lavishes itself on others. You can see the love that seeketh not its own in the missionary, regardless of comfort or health or money, laboring to uplift and save some sunken and degraded people; you can see it in the Salvation Sister living only to minister to people in their poverty and sin; you can see it in many a layman who lives not for what he can get but for what he can do. But what about us? Have we got this love? For he that loveth not knoweth not God. There is no real kinship between the selfish man and the God who for love's sake gave His Son. And therefore there can be no heaven for the selfish man. In Mr. Studdert Kennedy's latest book there is this striking little poem on a man selfish even in his religion:

> I would buy me a perfect Island Home,
> Sweet set in a southern sea,

And there I would build a Paradise,
For the heart of my Love and me.
I would plant me a perfect garden there,
The one that my dream soul knows,
And the years would flow as the petals grow,
That flame to a perfect rose.
I would build me a perfect temple there,
A shrine where my Christ might dwell.
And then you would wake to behold your soul
Damned deep in a perfect Hell.

That is true—the self-seeking, self-centered soul finds hell, not heaven. Heaven is the abode of love, and love is the qualification for entrance. I read the Gospels and I find that the people who practiced the love that seeketh not its own have an abundant entrance ministered unto them, and are welcomed with Christ's "Come, ye blessed of my Father." We shall all want to hear that welcome at the last. Then let us practice love. Let us follow Christ into the field of ministry. Let us live not for self, but for the good we can do. It will bring us to heaven at the last, but long before heaven is reached we shall discover that it is more blessed to give than to receive.

CHAPTER SIX

The Qualities of Love—Part 4

Love is not provoked; taketh not account of evil;
rejoiceth not in unrighteousness, but rejoiceth with the
truth.   *—1 Corinthians 13:5–6*

Love is never irritated, never resentful; love is never
glad when others go wrong; love is gladdened by
goodness.   *—1 Corinthians 13:5–6 MOFFATT*

We must not imagine as we read this chapter that the various qualities the apostle assigns to love are set down anyhow, casually, at random, just as they occurred to the apostle's mind. Paul's mind was an enormously fertile mind, but it was also an orderly and consecutive mind. If you will only brood over these various attributes of love as the apostle sets them down you will find that they follow one another in a certain natural sequence of thought. The first of the phrases we are to consider together this morning illustrates the truth of what I am saying. The series of phrases which I have read out as my text, taken together, may be said, as Mr. Percy Ainsworth suggests, to describe love's attitude in face of wrong. The first thing Paul says about love in this connection is that it is "not provoked." But I cannot bring myself to feel that that is at all an adequate translation of the words of the original. I suppose the revisers clung to the word *provoked* because it had been made familiar and dear by the KJV rendering. I think they would have been better advised to choose another word altogether. I am not sure indeed that the KJV rendering, "is not easily provoked," does not really come nearer to the apostle's meaning, although in the original Greek there is no separate word for "easily." Because the idea of quick blazing into wrath is certainly in the verb Paul uses. Love is often "provoked," but it is not swift to flame up into anger. "Love is not irritated," is Moffatt's translation. It does not allow itself to be exasperated. I should be inclined to substitute an adjective for the verb and say "Love is not irritable," and I am quite sure I would not be far from the apostle's meaning. Now I want you to notice how this quality of love springs out of the preceding one: "Love seeketh not its own." I said in the preceding sermon that the fact that "love seeketh not its own" gave the reason for the previous assertion that love "doth not behave itself unseemly," "love is never rude." The Corinthians by their pushfulness and self-assertiveness had introduced confusion and disorder into the services of the church, and were bringing its worship into contempt. In the next chapter the apostle lays down certain broad rules about the conduct of worship. But the real cure for the unseemliness of conduct was not to be found in the laying down of rules but in the spread of the spirit of love. Rules might be broken, but love would be an effectual remedy. Love would never behave itself unseemly for the simple reason that love seeketh not its own. Love is never self-assertive: love is always self-forgetful and self-sacrificing.

But that same truth about love—that it seeketh not its own—is also the secret of the quality which the apostle mentions next—love is not irritable. For why do people get irritable and querulous? Why did these people in the Corinthian church blaze out into fierce anger? Because their pride was injured and their vanity hurt because some other member insisted upon exercising his gift when they wanted to display theirs. All the quarrelling, all the friction, all the bad temper sprang from self-assertiveness. But if the love that seeketh not its own were enthroned in their hearts, all their swiftness to take offense would entirely disappear. It is always the self-centered people who are touchy, testy, and easily provoked. But love, just because it seeketh not its own, is not irritable.

The Sweet Temper of Love

Love is not irritable. There are all kinds of little annoyances and petty injustices in life which have it in their power to irritate us if we will allow them. But love has a way of ignoring pinpricks, and keeping calm and sweet and good-natured in spite of them all. That does not mean that love cannot be angry. Love would not be holy love at all if it could not be angry. Love ought to be and is a flame of fire against injustice and wrong. I said in a previous sermon that the love of God in Christ is the primal and pattern love. Well, do we not read sentences like this: "He," Jesus, "looked round about upon them with anger"? And do we not read about "the wrath of the Lamb"? Love and wrath are not exclusives. That is not love which smiles fatuously at wrong and does nothing. No parent loves his child who sees him committing sin and spares the rod. The capacity for a holy wrath is an element in real love. God's wrath, as some one has said, is just His love on fire. This apostle who says here that love is not irritable in another passage allows a righteous anger. But there is all the difference in the world between righteous anger at wrong, and irritability over every small grievance and inconvenience. Love is capable of the one, but is absolutely incapable of the other. Love is not irritable. Love is not swift to take offense.

But isn't irritability very much a matter of original disposition? Doesn't it largely depend upon temperament? Do not some men seem to be born with what we call good tempers and others with hot and inflammable tempers? Yes, that is so. Some people are far more placid and equable than others. They are not so inflammable. It is the difference between the phlegmatic and the choleric temperaments. Isn't there a story of a clergyman who one day fell into a passion and one of his churchwardens rebuked him and said he ought to control his temper. "Sir," replied the clergyman, "I control more temper in five minutes than you do in five years." There is undoubtedly that difference between people. Some are much more prone to be irritable than others. Theirs, shall I say, is a low flash point. But that is no excuse for giving way to irritation. It may be a harder business for some than for others, but temper can be schooled and disciplined and tamed. We know of people in whom it has been so schooled and disciplined and tamed. We have instances in this book. I imagine John was a fierce-tempered person in his youth. He got his name "Boanerges" because he was so passionate. You see the kind of person John was in the story that tells us he wanted to call down fire from heaven upon some Samaritan villagers who refused to give hospitality to Jesus. That was the original John—a man with a temper like a flame. But the John of later days was a man whose heart overflowed with kindness and affection. They knew him throughout the church as the Apostle of Love. Love tamed his temper, and made him a man of infinite patience and graciousness. I do not think that Paul was naturally a man of placid temperament. I think there were capacities for flaming anger in Paul. Once they broke out, as when after being struck on the mouth at the command of Ananias, the highpriest, he cried, "God shall smite thee, thou whited wall," but it was only for a moment. Swift on the heels of that outburst came the apology; Paul was ashamed of that moment's irritation. His rule was not to avenge himself, but to give place unto wrath. Temper had been so schooled and disciplined in Paul that he had become one of the most patient of men. And love had been his teacher, for love is not irritable. We are apt to regard irritability as a venial fault and not as a sin. But it is responsible for a vast proportion of the misery and unhappiness of the world. The peculiarity of ill temper, Drummond says, is that it is the vice of the virtuous. There are men and women who would be all but perfect were it not that they are easily ruffled, touchy, quick tempered. And it is the vice of the virtuous because we have not really regarded it as a vice. We have thought of it rather as a failing than as a sin. The truth is, Drummond further says, there are two great classes of sins—sins of the body and sins of the disposition. We have no doubt at all as to which of these classes of sins is the worse. It is on sins of the body we visit our heaviest condemnation. But are we right? We brand drunkenness and impurity as heinous sins and so indeed they are. But are they worse than sins of the disposition like avarice and bad temper? We have both classes of sins pictured for us in the parable of the prodigal son. The younger son stands for the sins of the flesh. He wasted his substance in riotous living. He devoured his father's living with harlots. They were grievous sins of which he was guilty, and he reaped the bitter fruit of them both in his body and in his soul. The elder son stands for the sins of disposition. No fault could be found with the elder brother's life. He had observed all the respectability and proprieties. He enjoyed a blameless reputation. But he had a jealous, sullen, and morose spirit. So when his younger brother came back, instead of joining in the general rejoicing, his bitter and jealous spirit revealed itself in churlish and sullen conduct. "He was angry and would not go in." It is not for us to say which is the greater sin—the self-indulgence of the younger brother, or the angry petulance of the elder. I wonder whether I am wrong in thinking that Jesus marks the conduct of the elder brother as the more grievous—for while we see the younger son, in spite of his sin, seated at the festal board, at the last view we get of the elder brother he is still outside—shut out by his own sulleness and irritability. Whether that be so or not, this is true—that the sin of the elder brother caused the greater misery. The younger brother was his own worst enemy: he sinned for the most part against himself. But the irritability and bad temper of the elder brother clouded everybody's sky and made everybody unhappy: his father, his brother, the guests at the feast, the servants; his ugly temper cast a gloom on the spirits of them all. Irritability is not something to be dismissed as a light and trivial thing. It is fraught with measureless powers of evil. Let me quote a couple of sentences from Drummond: "No form of vice, not worldliness, not greed of gold, not drunkenness itself, does more to un-Christianize society than evil temper. For embittering life, for breaking up communities, for destroying the most sacred relationship, for devastating homes, for withering up men and women, for taking the bloom off childhood, in short, for sheer gratuitous misery-producing power, this influence stands alone." That is strongly stated, but it is not overstated. I read a story the other day of a poor woman whose whole life was embittered and made a burden by the irritable temper of her husband. The constant rasp of his angry speech broke her down both in body and in soul. He was a blight even on the workshop in which he labored. But there is no need to go to fiction for proof and illustration. Don't we know from experience the misery an irritable person may create? He is like grit in the machine, causing infinite friction. I have seen the irritable man create trouble in the church. I have seen him make a committee miserably uncomfortable. I have seen him turn the home into a bear garden. Drummond is quite right: "For sheer gratuitous misery-producing power, bad temper, irritability stands alone." And the one cure for this devastating and desolating vice is love. To resolve to set a watch over one's lips so that the hot and hasty word shall never escape, is not enough. The spirit must be changed. And the only way to do that is to let Christ take possession of the heart. For when He takes possession of the heart, He fills it with his own Spirit. And His Spirit was one of uttermost love. Not only did He not allow the small injustices and petty grievances of life to change Him, but even the cruel and monstrous injuries of the Passion evoked no hot or angry word. When reviled, He reviled not again. Unwearied in forgiveness still, His heart could only love. And when He comes He will fill our hearts with a love like His own, and love will make us patient and forbearing and gentle. For love is not irritable.

Love and Memory

The next phrase of my text sets forth another exquisitely beautiful quality of love—love "taketh not account of evil." The KJV rendering, "Love thinketh no evil," misses the point. Love is a pure and holy thing and it is nothing wonderful at all to say, "love thinketh no evil." Love, just because it is love, would never dream of plotting ill against anybody, or cherishing evil thoughts about anybody. To say that would be to utter the veriest truism. But what Paul says here is not that love never plots or plans evil itself, but that it takes no account of evil committed against itself. What the apostle means is that the man who has love in his heart not only never dreams of wronging anybody else, but even when someone has wronged him he takes no account of it. He doesn't keep it in his memory. He erases it from the tablets of his mind. He doesn't reckon it. The words conjure up the picture of a man keeping an account book and certain things are not entered in the account book at all. Love doesn't enter in the account book wrongs and injuries and unkindness. Love taketh not account of evil. The account book which we all of us keep is the account book of memory. Now we have more control over memory than we sometimes imagine. We have a phrase about memory being like a sieve. Well, it is like a sieve in this respect, that it lets some things through and it keeps others. And we decide what it shall keep. We select our memories. By attention and letting our mind dwell upon them, we fix certain things upon our memories. Well, what do the account books of memory contain? Some people brood over slights, and injustices, and injuries done to them. You find these things scored and underlined in their memories. It is tragic to find, for example, David on his dying bed recalling the wrongs that Joab had done him, and hearing again the curses Shimei showered upon him as he fled from Jerusalem. David had got these things all written down in his account books. But you will not find these things in the account books of love. Love taketh no account of evil. It makes no entry of them. That is true of the account books of God. Indeed, our very salvation depends on that very fact. If all the evil we do were strictly entered up, and then brought in evidence against us, what chance should we have? If God were strict to mark iniquity, which of us should stand? But that is the wonderful thing about God—He taketh not account of evil. The Recording Angel carefully puts all our evil deeds down, and every day tells its tale of shortcoming and sin. But when the books are opened and the inquiry made, What is there against so-and-so and so-and-so? Against you and against me? The amazing answer is "Nothing"! Nothing! We sinful people are treated as if we were completely righteous people. There is no condemnation to them that are in Christ Jesus. God taketh not account of evil. He keeps strict account of every little deed of good things that slip our memory—little deeds of kindness to the poor, visits paid to the sick, words of sympathy spoken to the lonely and the bereaved; every one of those is remembered and carefully set down to our credit. But no record is kept of our evil deeds. And yet we did them; our own consciences bear witness against us. We sinned and came short of the glory of God. Every day we grieved Him by rebelling against Him. What has become of these our manifold sins and wickedness—multitudinous almost as the sands of the sea? Well, this is what has happened to them. God has erased them. With the blood of His dear and only Son He has wiped them out: "I have blotted out as a thick cloud thy transgressions and as a cloud thy sins." God's infinite love taketh not account of evil.

And so far as love is in our hearts it will be the same also with us. If I may go back to the parable of the Prodigal, for example—it is the elder brother, the man with the hard and sullen spirit, who rakes up the Prodigal's evil past. "This, thy son," he said, "which hath devoured thy living with harlots"—the bitter heart never forgets the ugly things; but there is no mention of the Prodigal's sin in any word the father said. In his speech there was nothing but affection and loving welcome, "This, my son, was dead and is alive again." Love taketh not account of evil. Well, what about this quality of love? Do we possess it? What do we keep in our memories? The slight people have offered to us? The supposed injuries they have done us? Is it the bad and bitter things we brood over and remember? Or have we the love that makes us wipe these things off the tablets of our memories and remember only the best about them? *De mortuis nihil nisi bonum.* "Concerning the dead nothing but what is good." But we ought not to wait till people are dead before we practice that rule. It is a rule for life. They used to say about Abraham Lincoln that he never forgot a kindness, but that he hadn't room in his mind for the memory of a wrong. That ought to be true of all Christian people. For Christian people are people in whom the love of Christ has been shed abroad. And this is the very mark of love—it taketh not account of evil. In a word it forgives and forgets. How do we stand the test? What do we keep in the records of our memories? People have hurt you and grieved you and offended you? Do you still count it against them? Or have you forgiven? There is only one thing that can stay the erasing hand of God, and that is the refusal on our part to forgive wrongs done to us. "If we forgive not men their trespasses neither will your Father forgive us our trespasses." One of the things—perhaps the only thing—that finally closes the doors of heaven against a man is the unforgiving spirit. For heaven is the abode of love. Love is the qualification for entrance. And this is one unfailing mark of love: It taketh not account of evil.

Love and Evil Report

And now for the third mark of love when face-to-face with evil. It doesn't allow itself to be irritated by the petty annoyances of life; it does not keep in memory wrongs done to itself; and, thirdly, it has no malicious pleasure in hearing of the failure and wickedness of other people, even though such failure and wickedness do not directly concern itself. "Love rejoiceth not in unrighteousness." Or, as Moffatt vividly translates it, bringing out the thought that is in the apostle's mind, "Love is never glad when others go wrong." But is anyone glad when others go wrong? Does anyone take an evil pleasure in hearing of the failure and breakdown of other people? What answer are you going to give to a question like that? Alas, my brethren, I know of no reflection upon human nature more damaging than this, that we take an ugly delight in hearing of the misdeeds and moral failures of people! There has been a vast amount of smacking of the lips over the unsavory disclosures recently made in our law courts. People have taken a malicious pleasure in reading of the ghastly immoralities of so-called society folk. I don't know why we should find this perverted pleasure in reading of the wickedness of others, unless it is that it makes us a bit more satisfied with ourselves. Anyhow, there the dreadful fact stands—final and convincing proof of original sin—that people do find some sort of ugly and detestable pleasure in the breakdown and shame of other folk. But love is never glad when others go wrong. Love takes no delight in hearing of men's sins and shames and follies. If you want to know what love delights in, you have it in the next phrase, it rejoices with the truth, or, as Dr. Moffatt translates it, "love is gladdened by goodness." If a man has an evil thing to say about another, love will not hear it. If a man has a good thing to say about another, love is an eager listener. Love finds no satisfaction in hearing of a man's sin, love mourns and weeps over that. Do you want illustration and proof of it? Well, recall how Love Incarnate behaved itself in the presence of sin. They brought to Him a wretched woman one day who had forgotten all her vows, and who had sacrificed personal purity and family happiness on the altar of unholy passion. The scribes and Pharisees who thrust the poor creature into His presence with a sort of evil and brutal delight shouted out her shame and gloated over her downfall. But Jesus took no pleasure in unrighteousness. He found no sort of pleasure in the fact that a fellow creature had gone wrong. The tragedy of it all filled Him with sorrow that amounted to agony. He was ashamed for the woman and ashamed for her accusers, and to hide the burning blush of shame that suffused His cheek He stooped and began writing in the sand. Evil moved Jesus to grief and tears: "When He beheld the city He wept over it." He was never glad when others went wrong, but He was gladdened by goodness. He rejoiced with the truth. He had a deep and holy pleasure when He saw signs of reviving goodness in an evil heart. When He saw the beginnings of faith in the Samaritan woman He was so rejoiced that He was lifted clean above all bodily weariness. "I have meat to eat," He said to His amazed disciples, "that ye know not of." When He saw the flower of generosity springing up in the hard soil of Zacchaeus's heart, He said with something like exultation in His voice, "This day is salvation come to this house." Jesus was made glad by goodness. "There is joy in the presence of the angels of God over one sinner that repenteth." Not over the sin—that fills heaven with pain—but over the sinner that repents, the sinner in whose heart there appears the first uprising of goodness. That was how Incarnate Love acted. He was gladdened by goodness, but sin and evil moved Him to such grief and shame that at last they broke His heart.

Well, how fares it with us? Love is never glad when others go wrong, love is gladdened by goodness. Do we bear this mark? What did you do with that last ugly story you heard? Lock it up in your breast, weep over it, pray over it? Or did you relate the story to the first person you met as a tidbit of news? It is a damning comment upon us that we take an evil delight in scandal, and that to so many an ugly story about someone else is a sweet morsel. But that is not love's way. You remember how the knights of King Arthur's table were pledged to "speak no slander, no, nor listen to it." That is love's law. Do we observe it? Love is never glad when others go wrong; love is gladdened by goodness. Love rejoiceth not in unrighteousness, but rejoiceth with the truth.

CHAPTER SEVEN

The Qualities of Love—Part 5

Love beareth all things, believeth all things, hopeth all things, endureth all things. —1 Corinthians 13:7

The apostle in the last three verses we have studied together has occupied himself in setting down some of the shining qualities of love. In this verse he brings that particular part of his subject to a close with a series of daring, sweeping, comprehensive assertions. Just exactly as the writer of the great Epistle to the Hebrews in that magnificent chapter in which he gives us the roll call of the heroes of faith, comes to a point when in the interests of conciseness and brevity he feels he must bring his glorious recital to a finish, and so breaks off with the exclamation, "And what shall I more say? for the time would fail me to tell of Gideon, Barak, Samson, Jephthah, of David and Samuel and the prophets," and then concludes with a general reference to those who through faith had subdued kingdoms, wrought righteousness, stopped the mouths of lions, waxed mighty in war, and put to flight armies of aliens. At this point Paul, feeling that the enumeration of the qualities of love would be an endless business, sums it all up and brings his analysis to an end in this series of startling, sweeping assertions—"love beareth all things, believeth all things, hopeth all things, endureth all things." The repetition of those words "all things" in each clause, seems to me to be significant. Hitherto the apostle has been discussing love's behavior in particular circumstances. Here he seems to be thinking of love's attitude towards the total sum of things. Confronting life with its sorrows and pains and the universe with its problems, love has a look of shining courage on its face, it beareth, believeth, hopeth, endureth all things.

Mr. Percy Ainsworth heads the chapter in which he discusses this particular verse, "The Optimism of Love." And in so entitling it, he has correctly described the contents of this verse. For what Paul here asserts is that love faces the wrongs and miseries and injuries of life, and the tangled problems of this baffling world, with a high courage and an indomitable hopefulness. It looks steadily at what Whittier calls "this perplexing maze of things," and it bates no jot of heart or hope. Love is bravely, invincibly optimistic. Only, as Mr. Ainsworth himself says, when we say that love is optimistic, we must be quite sure that we know what we mean by optimism. Much that passes for optimism in our days is not love's optimism at all. There is nothing cheap or shallow or easy about love's optimism, and a good deal that passes for optimism is as cheap and shallow as it can be made. There is, for example, the optimism of the man who is resolutely determined always to look on the bright side of things. And looking on the bright side of things for him amounts to a stubborn refusal to see that there is a dark side at all. Every cloud, he says, has a silver lining, and he is so intent upon the silver lining that he denies the existence of the cloud altogether. He is resolved, like Mark Tapley, to be jolly in all circumstances.

"Let's be happy," he says; "we live in a good world." That is a kind of optimism gained by a deliberate suppression of the truth. It is an optimism only maintained by shutting the eyes to plain and obvious facts. But of what use is an optimism of that kind? I suppose it is possible for a man to persuade himself that this is a cheerful world, if he excludes from his purview everything that is unpleasant and horrid and tragic. That ancient Persian monarch of whom the old Book speaks tried to delude himself into the belief that the world was a happy world by refusing to allow anyone clothed in sackcloth—dressed in mourning, as we might say—to come near his palace gate. When Marie Antoinette came to Paris as a bride, they didn't allow a single ragged or starving person to appear on the streets along which the splendid procession passed. France was seething with discontent at the time, discontent born of dire poverty, a discontent which later broke out into the horrors of the Revolution, but Marie Antoinette was not to know anything about that. So the poor starving populace were swept into the side streets where they could not be seen, and kept penned up there so that Marie Antoinette might think all was happy and prosperous in Paris. But an optimism based on ignorance is not optimism at all. An optimism gained by a deliberate refusal to face the facts is not optimism but self-deception. It is a pitiful game of make-believe. It is playing blindman's buff with life. Optimism when it is the real thing is a noble grace; but this shallow thing which closes its eyes to the sorrows and sins, the tragedies and despairs of life is a particularly mean and ugly vice. For what is optimism? It is the reasoned and settled conviction— not that everything is all right—but that the ultimate meaning of things is good. It is the belief arrived at—after a frank facing of the facts—that, to use Emerson's phrase, things in this universe are arranged for truth and benefit. Such a conviction as that is not easily gained, nor is it to be held without effort. I refuse to call him an optimist who prates about everything being as it should be in this the best possible of worlds, as if he had never heard of sorrow or sin or pain or heartbreak or death. An honest laugh is a good gift of God, but the laughter of self-deluding fools of that sort is, as the old Book says in a sentence that is almost savage, "like the crackling of thorns under the pot." I have infinitely more respect for the pessimist than I have for the shallow-pated optimist. For at any rate the pessimist has faced the facts. He has opened his eyes to the existence of the slum and the sweating worker, and the stunted child, to the facts of poverty and strife and ruthless war, to pain and misery and death. They have so burned themselves into his soul that the world seems to him not all right, but all wrong, and he speaks bitterly of life. This man with his somber, despairing judgment of the world is far nearer the truth than the man who cackles and giggles his way through life, pretending that everything is exactly as it should be. The pessimist sees more deeply than the shallow optimist. And yet he does not see deeply enough. I remember reading a sermon of Philips Brooks (over thirty years ago now) in which he divided men—in respect of their attitude towards life—into three classes, the shallow optimists, the pessimists, the real optimists. I am not sure that he did not suggest that most men pass through all three stages in their own experience. We start life by being optimists. Everything looks happy to the normal child. As we grow older, however, we find life is full of trials and disappointments and disillusionment, and then we become pessimists. But as life proceeds we find that these trials and difficulties have their compensations, and contribute to the enrichment of life; and so we become optimists again—not the happy unthinking optimists of childhood, but serious optimists because convinced that behind life's varied experiences stands God, causing "all things to work together for good." Whether we all pass through these three stages or not, these three types of men exist—the shallow optimist, the pessimist, the real optimist. Now I repeat, the pessimist is much nearer the truth than the shallow optimist, for he has faced the facts. But he has not faced all the facts, and he has not penetrated to the ultimate truth. To use an illustration Philips Brooks employs in that sermon—the surface of the earth is warmed by the direct rays of the sun. But below the warm surface, the earth is cold and dank and dark and dreary. But penetrate deeper, and you get to the warmth again, warmth supplied by the earth's central and essential heart. And so there is the surface sight of life which is bright and happy. And then there is the sight which looks beneath the surface and which sees all manner of mean and ugly and dreadful things. Then there is the deepest sight of all which sees something warm and gracious at the very heart of things. It is only this latter and deepest sight which will make a man a genuine optimist. I do not know that the bare facts of life will make him one—though philosophers have argued that on the balance life is good—for wrong and suffering and sorrow are so obtrusive. The only thing that will make a man genuinely optimistic—believing that good shall be the final goal of ill—is to see behind all the tragic facts of life a loving God. The type of the genuine optimist is our Lord Jesus Himself. There was nothing shallow or superficial about Him. He did not blind Himself to the sin and sorrow of the world. He did not pretend that everything was all right. It was because things had gone so tragically wrong that He came into our world at all. The weight of the world's woe was forever on His heart. He knew quite well that the world had gone so tragically wrong, that for the climax of its wickedness it would nail Him to the accursed tree. And yet in spite of rejection and shame and death—ignoring nothing and closing His eyes to nothing, Jesus remained quietly, serenely confident. "Be of good cheer," He said at the darkest moment of His midnight, "I have overcome the world." And if you ask me for the secret of our Lord's optimism, I reply that you will find it in His absolute certainty of God—the living, loving, redeeming God. And that is the secret of real optimism still—to know that God is at work. "Hope thou in God," said the psalmist, "for I shall yet praise Him who is the health of my countenance and my God." That is the only way to courage and high confidence as we face this tangled world, and our own perplexed and perplexing lives.

Now you may think that in saying all this I have wandered far away from my text. But in reality, I do not think I have. For that is exactly the kind of optimism which my text suggests. It is quite clearly not the shallow optimism that ignores the tragedy of life, and refuses to acknowledge that anything is wrong. Look at the verbs in the first and last clauses, "love beareth all things," "love endureth all things." The very words suggest that love—if you will allow me the phrase—is "up against things." There are burdens that have to be borne, there are things that test endurance almost to the breaking point. There is no pretending that life is smooth and easy. Love is never blind—love is open-eyed. Love recognizes that life is oftentimes terribly hard and difficult. But though love is up against things and ignores none of the harshness and trials of life, it yet keeps a brave heart; it believeth all things, it hopeth all things. In face of the worst it believes in the best. And love is possessed of this high courage because it looks up to God, before it looks out upon the world and upon men. For this love of which the apostle speaks is not ἔρως, the love of passion, that earthly and sensual love; it is ἀγάπη, that serene and sacred and holy love which is born of God, and looks up to God, before it looks out upon men. And that is why love, though bearing on its heart the hardships and difficulties, the wrongs and injuries of which life is full, yet believeth and hopeth all things—it has looked upon the face of God before it has looked out upon the world.

Now for a few minutes further let me examine briefly the various phrases which the apostle uses to describe the optimism of love.

Love Bearing all Things

The first thing he says is this: "Love beareth all things." Those of you who use the RV will notice that in the margin the translation "covereth" is suggested. "Love covereth all things." Love doesn't talk about other people's wrongs and failings, it hides them and casts a veil over them. Of course, that makes quite good sense and it sets forth a real quality of love. But that particular aspect of love has already been spoken of in the phrase, "love taketh not account of evil," "rejoiceth not in unrighteousness." So that the Revisers were probably right in sticking to the translation "beareth" in the text, especially as in another chapter of this epistle where the word is also used, "bear" is the only possible translation. "Love beareth all things," says the apostle. And Dr. Edwards in his commentary says that that means "bears without resentment injuries inflicted by others." Love does not break out into fierce and uncontrollable outbursts of passion under wrong—love beareth all things. Love does not become frantic and rebellious in face of sorrow and grief—love beareth all things. A noble forbearance and self-restraint is one of the marks of love. It does not flame out into resentment against the injurer, it does not seek to avenge the wrong, it bears things with a brave patience because it knows there is a God that judgeth righteously. It does not break out into frantic rebellion in face of loss and pain. It bears things with a noble submission, because it knows that the Lord gives and the Lord takes away, and that blessed always is the name of the Lord. Love that has looked upon the face of God beareth all things.

But I do not think the reference is to be confined to our own injuries and troubles and griefs. Love beareth *all* things. Love bears the weight and burden of the world's misery and sin. Love does not try to escape this load by refusing to contemplate the woe of the world. Love deliberately faces it all, and bears it. And when I say that love bears it, I do not mean to suggest that love acquiesces in the misery and evil. Love does not fold its hands and do nothing. Love seeks by every means to lessen the world's evil, and abolish the world's misery. Love has been the impulse behind every ameliorating movement. But love does not get fretful or rebellious or frantic. There are some men who become almost frantic because of the ills from which mankind suffers. They revolt against the system which allows these ills to exist, and often by their revolt they only plunge their fellows into misery deeper still. But love beareth all things. It can bear the sight of the pain and misery of the world, without becoming either bitter or mad, because it has seen God. If you want to see love bearing all things, let your gaze rest on Jesus. He took on Himself the whole burden of the world's woe and sin. He bore our sins in His own body on the tree. And He bore it all without fretfulness or bitterness or impatience. When He suffered He threatened not, but committed Himself to Him that judgeth righteously. It is, as Mr. Ainsworth says, only on Calvary that we can find the last meaning of these calm, patient words, Love beareth all things.

Love Believing all Things

Love, the apostle goes on to say, "believeth all things." And that means "that love is ever disposed to believe the best of men. There are some people who always put the worst possible construction upon the actions of their fellows. They seem incapable of believing in disinterested goodness. They think that behind every generous deed there is some selfish motive. If a man does some big thing for his town or country they always want to know what he is going to get out of it. There are plenty of evil-minded people who refuse to believe in the real goodness of any man, or the purity of any woman. They belittle and besmear their kind. I suppose it is that they judge every one by their own mean and selfish minds. To the pure all things are pure, says the old Book—but to the selfish all things and people are selfish, and to the base all things and people are base, and to the unclean all things and people are unclean. Our judgments are projections and reflections of ourselves.

And the mean and selfish man is bound to be a pessimist because it is only mean and base and sordid motives he sees at work in the world. But love believeth all things. It believes the best about a man. And that is not because love is credulous. Love, as I have again and again reiterated, is not blind; love is insight. Love indeed is the condition of true vision. Love is the condition of understanding anything. You must love art to understand art. You must love music to understand music. You must love poetry to appreciate poetry. It is of no use expecting a man with no love of art to appreciate Raphael, or a man with no love of music to appreciate Beethoven, or a man with no love of poetry to appreciate Shelley or Keats. And in exactly the same way you must have love for men if you are to understand them. It is of no use expecting a man with no love in his soul to appreciate men. His gaze will be held by surface appearances—by the rough and repellent exterior. It takes love to penetrate to the hidden splendor. Why, we have known people in our own experience who, by men who only knew them casually, might be written down as boors, but who to sympathetic and loving eyes revealed themselves as possessing hearts of gold. Love penetrates beneath the rough exterior, sees deeper than superficial faults and failings, sees deep down in the heart of man capacities for nobility, instincts for holiness, a hunger for God. They are there in every man, buried deep sometimes, but not buried so deep that love cannot see them.

How that hidden splendor flashed before our astonished eyes in those tragic years of war. In the commonest clay we saw, there were embedded glorious capabilities of heroism and self-sacrifice. Love sees all that. And because it sees it, it believeth all things. Wasn't that the characteristic of Love Incarnate? Jesus believed the best of people. He believed the best of people whom everybody else regarded as hopelessly degraded and vile. It was because He saw hidden splendors, infinite capabilities buried in the hearts of the outcasts of Palestine, that He became the friend of publicans and sinners. He was optimistic even about them; he believed good things about them. And the belief He had in them was a factor in their salvation. Simon began to believe he would get rid of his vacillation and instability when he heard Jesus speak of him as the rock; publicans and sinners began to believe that goodness was possible even for them when they found that Jesus believed in them. Men are apt to respond to the faith folk have in them. If you believe in a man you help to make him worthy of your belief, for it becomes a point of honor with him to justify your faith in him. Contempt for a man helps to make him contemptible. Love, by believing the best of him, helps to make him good in actual fact. Love is optimistic about the world, because it is optimistic about human nature. Love believeth all things. And by its very optimism it tends to make men what it believes them to be. This love that believes in them becomes a challenge to them. As Mr. Ainsworth puts it in a fine sentence, "Through the tired ranks of the vanquished, through the throngs of the disheartened, across the trampled field of life strewn with wasted efforts and battered dreams, love passes, still believing all things. And in the light of that brave faith many a man stretches out his hand for his sword and finds it worth gripping, even though it be a broken one." That is true, men are saved by the faith that others have in them—by the love that believeth all things.

Love Hoping all Things

Love, the apostle goes on to say, "hopeth all things." Dr. Edwards' comment on this phrase runs as follows: "Love hopes even when it cannot find ground for faith." Hoping all things, is optimism carried a point higher than believing all things. There are people in whom love with all its keenness of insight cannot discern any signs of hidden splendor. Doesn't one of the apostles talk about people whose consciences appear to be seared as with a hot iron? Doesn't he speak of some as being "past feeling"? And of others as being "given up to a reprobate mind"? These are people in whom love with its keen but kindly eyes for all its searching could not discover ground for "believing" good things concerning them. And yet although it could not discover ground for faith, it continued to hope. It hoped that there was some good in them that it could not see. Love hopeth all things. Love casts none aside as worthless. It surrenders none as beyond redemption. No! it cannot give reasons for this courageous and optimistic attitude. But there it is—love hopeth all things. A mother hopes on for her prodigal son, though there may not be in the son's conduct a single sign to justify the hope. Friends, acquaintances, neighbors have long since despaired of him. But love hopes on. And that is how it is with all in whose hearts love dwells—they have hope for the worst—they hope when there is no hint or promise of amendment. I suppose that back of love's hopefulness, and justifying it, is the fact that on the one hand God is seeking man, and on the other that man is made for God. And so love never despairs of anybody. Love hopeth all things. And as it hopes all things for the individual so it hopes all things for the world. There are times when to take a cheerful view of the future seems sheer folly. Every fact seems to challenge the optimistic view. All the signs seem to justify and warrant the most gloomy prognostications of the most gloomy pessimists. We are living in such a time just now. We seem to be heading not for the Parliament of man and the federation of the world but for Armageddon. All our public men utter solemn and somber warnings that unless things change our civilization will go crashing into ruin. And yet love, looking up to God on the one hand, and believing in the ultimate goodness of the human heart on the other, amid all the failures and disappointments and fears of these times, still hopeth all things and looks confidently for the dawning of the better day.

Love Enduring all Things

And the final thing that the apostle says about the optimism of love is that it "endureth all things." This word *endure* is a stronger word than the word *bear* in the first clause. It means that the spirit is not crushed under the weight of heaviest affliction and disappointment. This is Dr. Edwards' comment on this final clause, "Love endures even when it fails to hope." This is the very climax of love's courage and indomitable optimism—it hopes when it cannot find ground for faith, it endures even when it cannot find ground for hope. Love endureth all things. Love stands its ground. Love never yields. Love never surrenders. No sorrow, no defeat, no set-back can destroy its optimism. It endures even when every chance seems gone. Love is like a soldier set at a certain post. The battle sweeps and swirls around him. Defeat seems to have overtaken the armies to which he belongs. It seems useless to hold on to that post. But his general has set him there—and there he will stay until he is recalled. Love is like that. It holds its ground in the day of defeat. It keeps its face to the dawn even at darkest midnight. It endureth all things. Jesus speaking of the difficulties and trials that beset a man in the Christian life said, "He that endureth to the end shall be saved." Love has that enduring quality. It never fails or breaks. Love holds on when others faint and give way. Multitudes have taken a hand in the great work of creating a better world. They have been animated by social enthusiasm, by sentimental pity, by concern for the safety of the state. But many of those have grown weary in well doing; they have been chilled by disappointment, soured by disillusionment. But love—the love that looks up to God and then out upon man endures all things, clings to its task in spite of disappointment, persists in its labors in spite of all delays. It never falters, it never staggers at the promise because of unbelief. It holds on. It keeps its courage high. And when at last the new earth is created, it will be this love, this believing, hoping, indomitable love enduring all things—that will have brought it to pass.

CHAPTER EIGHT

The Permanence of Love

Love never faileth: but whether there be prophecies,
they shall be done away: whether there be tongues, they
shall cease: whether there be knowledge, it shall be
done away. —*1 Corinthians 13:8*

When I began my exposition of this wonderful chapter, I said that it fell quite naturally into three sections. In the first the apostle declares that without love all other gifts are worthless. In the second he describes the various qualities of love. In the third he asserts the supremacy of love over all other gifts because love is permanent and abiding. It is this third section—in which the apostle sings of love's permanence—that we are now to study together.

The apostle opens the section with a statement even more daring and sweeping than the uncompromising statements contained in the previous verse. In that verse he had said tremendous things about love. "Love," he had said, "beareth all things, believeth all things, hopeth all things, endureth all things." In spite of disappointments, disillusionment, defeats, adverse circumstances, love bears up and loves on. It is a picture of love's glorious and indomitable optimism. In the opening sentence of this section the apostle seems to be continuing the thought of the previous verse, carrying the daring of his claims for love to a point higher still. "Love," he says, "never faileth."

Dr. T. C. Edwards, indeed, says that the thought in this clause is

suggested by that word "endureth" in the preceding sentence. And,
taken by itself, the little phrase would serve for another touch in the
picture of the qualities of love. It adds the final and finishing touch
of splendor to it—"love never faileth." The word translated, *faileth*
means literally to "fall to the ground." Love never "falls out"; love
never "falls to the ground." The picture the word summons up
before my mental vision is that of a company of soldiers marching
through the heat in some tropic land. And as the weary miles lengthen
out and as the heat intensifies, exhausted nature reveals itself, and
one after another faints and falls by the way—until at last out of all
the company only one is left doggedly, patiently marching on. "Love
never falls out." Friends, acquaintances, one-time comrades may by
degrees drop away, worn out by disappointment—but love holds
on, love never fails.

That is always one of the characteristics of real love—it lasts.
The best love of all is the love of God in Christ. That is the pattern,
the ideal love. And this is one of the marks of the divine love—it
never fails. "Having loved his own which were in the world," says
one of the Evangelists, "he loved them unto the end." These disciples
of His who are described in that verse as "His own" grieved Him,
tried Him, misunderstood Him, disappointed Him, but He just kept
on loving them, loving all along. But you will make a vast mistake
if you think that word "end" refers simply to the end of our Lord's
earthly life. He loved them on through death. He loved them when
death was passed. He loves them still. "He loved them unto the
end!" That is true, but the end is never reached. "I am persuaded,"
wrote St. Paul, "that neither death nor life, nor things present, nor
things to come, nor height nor depth, nor any other creature shall be
able to separate us from the love of God which is in Christ Jesus our
Lord." We are creatures of this time-world and can only think in the
categories of space and time; we cannot help using finite words
when we attempt to describe infinite things. And when we use such
phrases as loving "to the end," "to the finish," "to the very last," we
really mean loving through time and into eternity—just keeping on
loving, loving all along. "Love never faileth." That is certainly true
of the love of God in Christ—for that, according to St. Paul, is what
we shall be doing in heaven itself, seeking to apprehend with all
saints what is the breadth and length, and height and depth of the
love of Christ which passeth knowledge. And it is true of human
love in so far as it partakes of the nature of this holy agapé of which

the apostle speaks in this chapter. That is the difference—at any rate one of the differences—between ϵρος, the love of passion, and ἀγαη, this sacred and holy love which is born of God. The love of passion dies, but this sacred and holy love endures. The one is like the flame of burning straw or paper—one fierce blaze and then all over. The other is like the steady continuous glow of the coal fire. We are confronted almost every day with the tragic ruin caused by the failure of the love of passion. But ἀγαη, this holy love of God burning with steady glow through all changes of age, through all changes of condition, loving on in poverty as in wealth, in age as in youth, in sickness as in health, is the fountain of the purest happiness on this earth. Love—true love—the thing that deserves the name of love, "never faileth." You perhaps remember that poem of Mrs. Barrett Browning which she entitled "Loved Once." She begins by asking herself which is of all earth's sounds the most lamentable— the sigh of misfortune, the high sharp notes of strife, the sob of the mourner, the fall of kisses on unanswering clay—and she comes to the conclusion that sad though these sounds are, the most lamentable sound of all is that of the words, "I loved once." And then she rebels against the phrase and challenges its truth.

> And who saith, "I loved once"?
> Not angels, whose clear eyes, love, love foresee,
> > Love, through eternity,
> And by To Love do apprehend To Be.
> Not God, called Love, His noble crown-name casting
> > A light too broad for blasting:
> The Great God changing not from everlasting,
> > Saith never, "I loved once."
>
> Oh, never is "Loved once."
> Thy Word, thou Victim-Christ, misprized friend!
> > Thy cross and curse may rend,
> But having loved Thou lovest to the end.
> This is man's saying—man's too weak to move
> > One sphered star above
> Man desecrates the eternal God-word Love
> > By his "No more" and "Once."

And she finishes up by refusing to admit that those who use the phrase "loved once" ever really loved at all.

"But love strikes one hour—Love! those never loved, Who dreamed that they loved once." And Mrs. Browning is right. "Love never faileth." That word *never* is, as Mr. Ainsworth says, "a long word. It cannot be written in all the years." In this context, however, there must be no attempt to limit the meaning of the word. It means exactly what it says. It looks clean beyond the bounds of time and space. It embraces eternity within its sweep. It is not a case simply of love lasting undimmed and unfaltering throughout life's little day. It is a case of love continuing when earth and time have been left behind and eternity has begun "The days of our years are three score years and ten," says the psalmist. That is the average of the length of our sojourn upon this earth and of our fellowship together. But when the earthly fellowship is broken, love does not cease. Love lives on—while there is one friend here and another yonder. And love will live on when up yonder dear ones find themselves together once again. "Love never faileth."

That is how God loves, as I have already said. Death makes no difference to Him. "I am the God of Abraham and of Isaac and of Jacob." The happy, friendly, loving relationship continues through the eternal years. Those friends of God had long disappeared from these earthly scenes, but God had them still in His keeping—they were still the objects of His love. And all true love is of God and possesses that eternal quality which belongs to the divine love itself. "Love never faileth." Beyond death as on this side of death, in eternity as in time, love goes on loving, loving all along. I wonder how in face of a statement like this anyone could ever have a doubt about the possibility of recognition in the eternal world. Scripture never seeks to prove it, it simply takes it for granted. But a sentence like this quite clearly implies it. For love is a personal relation, and it is a reciprocal relation. As the philosopher would say, it implies subject and object. It would be foolish to talk about such a personal thing as love if there, as here, we did not exist as persons. The fact of love ought to banish all hesitations and doubts on this point. For love is not temporal, it is eternal. Most of us have dear ones on the other side; we haven't ceased to love them and they have not ceased to love us. Love never faileth. It was a true instinct that made Charles Kingsley wish to have those three Latin words engraved on the stone which marked the place where he and his wife lay buried,

Amavimus, Amamus, Amabimus. "We have loved, we love, we shall love." We shall love! For love never faileth.

Now it was this very quality of eternity, inherent in love, that made it so vastly superior to those other gifts—those charismata—by which the Corinthians set such store. The Corinthians made a great fuss about the gift of tongues, and the gift of prophecy, and the gift of knowledge. They were proud and puffed up if they possessed the one or the other. They set little or no store by love. For they were jealous of one another, and they envied one another, and they divided themselves into factions with the result—to use the apostle's own vivid phrase—that they bit and wellnigh devoured one another. Love was a sort of Cinderella in Corinth, disregarded, ignored, and neglected. And yet the apostle declares that tongues and prophecy and knowledge were nothing compared to love. For the word *temporary* was written across the gifts on which they prided themselves so much. But love was eternal. They were doomed to pass, but love was permanent. Love was better worth having than either prophecy or tongues or knowledge—for love would last. He illustrates and enforces the superiority of love in a series of contrasts.

Love and Prophecy

First of all, he contrasts it with prophecy. Now prophecy was a gift which the apostle highly valued. I think of all the gifts he valued it most. For it was a gift that contributed to the edification of the church. That is almost the last word he says in the chapter succeeding this one in which he discusses the worship of the church. "Wherefore, my brethren," he says, "desire earnestly to prophesy." For prophecy is not to be understood in the sense of speaking of things to come. It is not so much foretelling as forth telling. The prophets in the early church were people who spoke under the inspiration of the Spirit of God. They were men who brought messages from God for the comfort and enlightenment of the people. They corresponded more or less to the preachers of our day, though in their case there was much more consciousness of immediate inspiration. Prophecy then, was a great and precious gift. And yet it is nothing compared to love—for "whether there be prophecies, they shall be done away"—"done away" in the sense of "being brought to an end." Now, in what sense will prophecies be done away? Well, it is quite obvious that prophecies in the sense of foretellings are done away when they are fulfilled. The Old

Testament, for example, is full of prophecies that have been done away. In Isaiah and Jeremiah you will find prophecies of judgment and doom. They were done away by their fulfillment in the Exile. In the second chapter of Isaiah you will find glowing prophecies of restoration: they were done away by their fulfillment in the Return. In all the prophets there were great anticipations of Messiah. They were done away by their fulfillment in the coming of Christ. In the nature of things every true prophecy in the course of time is done away, because in the process of time anticipation gets converted into fact. As Henry Drummond puts it, these Old Testament prophecies having been fulfilled, their work is finished; they have nothing more to do now in the world except to feed a devout man's faith.

And even when prophecy is interpreted in the sense of preaching—there will come a time when it shall be done away. It is a great thing to be a preacher. It is the greatest calling in the world. To be able to speak for Christ, and to be able so to speak as to sway the crowd and touch the heart and win men for Christ's allegiance—what a work it is! I am not surprised that pious Scotch and Welsh parents think it still the highest honor that could be bestowed upon a son of theirs—that God should call him to be a preacher. But even the preacher's work will be done away. In its very nature it is transient and temporary. Preaching presupposes an unconverted world. But I read of a time coming when the earth shall be full of the knowledge of the Lord as the waters cover the sea; when it shall be no longer necessary for a man to teach his brother saying, "Know the Lord" for all shall know Him from the least to the greatest of them. That day may be far off as yet, but it will come—that blessed day when Christ shall deliver up the kingdom to God, even the Father, and God shall be all in all. The job of the preacher will be finished then. There will no longer be any need of him. "Whether there be prophecies, they shall be done away."

Love and Tongues

"Whether there be tongues," the apostle goes on to say, "they shall cease." The gift of tongues was a gift of ecstatic speech. The apostle did not rate it very highly for the simple reason that the speech was unintelligible to the ordinary Christian, and did not therefore minister to his edification. In his own blunt and downright way he says that he would rather speak five words with his understanding, so as to instruct others also, than ten thousand in a tongue. And he goes so far as to forbid the exercise of this gift at all in the public worship of the church unless there was someone present who could interpret. The Corinthians, on the contrary, were inordinately proud of this particular gift. They rated it above prophecy. It was more startling, and therefore attracted more attention, and perhaps brought its possessor more glory. But of this gift, too, the apostle says that it is temporary, "Whether there be tongues, they shall cease." This particular gift of tongues was just a sign for the unbelieving—to constrain their attention to the church and its message. When the church had become sufficiently strong to command attention without these adventitious aids, they simply ceased. This strange, bizarre gift of speaking with tongues has disappeared because it ceased to be necessary or even useful. The Corinthians showed a curious lack of discernment in laying such stress upon tongues while neglecting love. They were neglecting the abiding for the transient; the permanent for the perishing. "Whether there be tongues, they shall cease." Suppose we give a wider meaning to the phrase and interpret it of languages in general (though, of course, that interpretation was not in the apostle's mind), it still remains true. "Whether there be tongues, they shall cease." Tongues are all the while ceasing. Living languages become dead languages, and some pass clean out of the knowledge of men. F. W. Robertson puts the question: Suppose a man had known fifty languages in the days of St. Paul, how many—or rather, how few— would be of use now? On Pentecost the assembled people heard the apostles speak in their own languages—Parthians and Medes and Elamites and the dwellers in Mesopotamia, in Judea and Cappadocia, in Pontus and in Asia. All these dialects are obsolete today. "Whether there be tongues, they shall cease." Nothing, indeed, in the history of the world is more striking than the temporary character of tongues. The language in which Paul wrote this letter—that Greek language which was the Corinthians' native speech—it has ceased. Latin, the language of Imperial Rome, the official language of the world—as a spoken language it has ceased. Indeed, the phenomenon of a ceasing language is one that can be witnessed within the limits of these islands of ours. The Greek language is losing its hold in Scotland. One of the religious problems of our day is caused by the disappearance of the Welsh language from the mining valleys and the industrial towns of South Wales. Fifty years ago those valleys were entirely Welsh, and the Welsh chapels supplied every religious need. But the Anglicizing process has been going on with immense rapidity. The old people are satisfied with the Welsh chapel, but the children no longer understand the language and in many cases there is no English chapel to meet their need. It may be a long time yet before the Welsh language becomes extinct and is known only through its literature, but the process of extinction is going on beneath our very eyes. "Whether there be tongues, they shall cease."

Love and Knowledge

"Whether there be knowledge, it shall be done away." There were those in Corinth who prided themselves on their knowledge. They felt they had an insight into the mysteries of the faith which was not given to others. They were the intellectuals of the church, the people who considered themselves above the rest in intelligence, and who rather looked down upon them in consequence. They, too, were neglecting the permanent for the temporary—for whether there be knowledge, it shall be done away. "Done away," the apostle means in the sense of being superseded and made obsolete.

Knowledge is progressive. There is no such thing as a stock of knowledge, fixed, defined and complete that when once a man mastered it he could feel that he knew all there was to be known. Knowledge is a growing, expanding, developing thing that the learned man of one day may be completely behind the times the next. There is scarcely need to illustrate the truth of this, it is so perfectly obvious. From certain points of view the schoolboy of today knows vastly more than the wisest of the ancient Greeks. The knowledge of one generation is the ignorance of the next. The schoolbooks of today are a bit of a puzzle to the folk who have left their schooldays forty years behind. Think of geography. It is not a bit of use producing a map of Europe ten years of age—almost every national boundary has been altered in the meantime. Or think of science. Darwin, Huxley, Tyndall, all of them are superseded and out of date.

Henry Drummond mentions a striking fact about the medical library in Edinburgh. When Sir James Simpson, the discoverer of chloroform, died, he was succeeded by his nephew. The new professor was asked by the librarian to go through the library and pick out those books on his subject which were no longer needed. And his reply to the librarian was this: "Take every textbook that is more than ten years old and put it down in the cellar." Knowledge is not static—it grows from more to more. It is constantly being done away. And as it is in the realm of secular knowledge, so is it also in the realm of religious knowledge. The learned theologian of a generation ago would find himself hopelessly out of date today. For in the interval the critic and the historian have been at work. They have given us a new view of the Bible; they have given us a new conception of the environment in which Jesus lived; they have given us a new apologetic in face of the new science. The knowledge of the theological professor of fifty years ago has literally been done away. It would not be counted knowledge at all, but ignorance. And not only is our knowledge of the facts connected with our religion a progressive thing, but our apprehension of religious truth is a growing thing too. We grow in grace, and in the knowledge of our Lord and Savior Jesus Christ. We get truer and larger views of God. We are the heirs of the Puritans, and we are rightly proud of our ancestry. But we have left the theology of the Puritans far behind. It no longer satisfies us. What was true in it we have absorbed, but we have passed beyond it. The knowledge of one age is constantly being superseded by that of the next. "Whether there be knowledge, it shall be done away."

There is no disparagement, you will notice, of prophecy and tongues and knowledge. They were good things in themselves. Their only fault is that they were temporary. They didn't last. Yet upon these things the Corinthians were priding themselves! It is strange how people pride themselves on transient and temporary things still. On wealth, though we know quite well that as we brought nothing into this world, so we can carry nothing out. On fame— though we know quite well that the judgments of earth do not carry with them the judgments of heaven, and that there are "first who shall be last and last who shall be first." On social position—though we all come at last to a coffin and six feet of earth. There is nothing wrong in these things, but we ought not to give our strength to them for the simple reason that they do not last. "Love not the world," said John, "neither the things that are in the world"; not because it is sinful, but "because the world passeth away and the lusts thereof." Nothing deserves the homage and devotion of the immortal soul except something which is itself immortal. That is why love is supreme above all other gifts. Love never fails. Love is imperishable. It is never outgrown. It never becomes obsolete. It is never done away with. It is as much at home in heaven as it is here upon the earth. It is the only permanent and abiding wealth of life. Riches, fame, position, knowledge, tongues, prophecy—they will all slip from our hands. But the love we practice and cherish we shall keep for the eternal life. For love is itself divine and eternal. To have love is already to possess the eternal life. Put these two verses together. "This is eternal life to know Thee, the only true God." "Every one that loveth is born of God and knoweth God, for God is love." To know God is life. And how are we to know Him? Just by loving! Every one that loveth is born of God and knoweth God, for God is love. To love God, to love one another—that is to know God and to be born of Him. That is to share His eternal life. That is to carry within ourselves the pledge and promise of immortality—for love never fails. Love is the supreme gift—for love is never lost. The love you gave and give your loved ones within the veil is not lost. They receive it and respond to it, and one day it will reunite you in blessed fellowship. The love you give your fellows is not lost. It will meet you again. "Inasmuch," Jesus will say, "as you did it to one of these least, ye did it unto Me." The love you give to God is not lost. It binds you to Him in gracious bonds that neither life nor death can sever. Wealth, position, fame—all these things pass. But the man who is rich in love is rich to all eternity. Therefore with all your getting in this mortal life get the loving heart.

CHAPTER NINE

The Partial and the Complete

*For we know in part, and we prophesy in part; but when
that which is perfect is come, that which is in part shall
be done away. When I was a child, I spake as a child, I
felt as a child, I thought as a child; now that I am
become a man, I have put away childish things. For now
we see in a mirror darkly; but then face to face: now I
know in part, but then shall I know even as also I have
been known.* ——*1 Corinthians 13:9–12*

Strictly speaking, these four verses have nothing to do with love,
which is the apostle's main theme in this chapter. They are really
meant to develop and illustrate the thought expressed in the previous
verse, that the gifts of tongues and prophecy and knowledge upon
which the Corinthians set such store were in their very nature transient
and temporary. The apostle's argument would lose nothing in
clearness; possibly, indeed, it would gain, if we read straight on
from verse 8 to verse 13. "Whether there be prophecies, they shall
be done away: whether there be tongues, they shall cease: whether
there be knowledge, it shall be done away. But now abideth faith,
hope, love, these three; and the greatest of these is love." The
intermediate verses form a sort of parenthesis and are, as Dr.
Maclaren puts it, inserted to form a "buttress" in support of the
apostle's statement that knowledge and prophecy are being done
away. But though they have no direct bearing upon love, they are

worth studying for their own sake, and I make no apology for making them the subject of a separate sermon.

Before I begin my exposition, it is perhaps worthwhile to call your attention to the fact that the apostle drops all reference to the gift of tongues. Knowledge and prophecy will be done away with, he says, because they are continually being absorbed in something better. But there is no future for this gift of tongues. As Dr. Charles Edwards expresses it, "ecstatic speech is not an imperfect stage capable of being developed into a higher form. It will cease entirely, much as sounds which have no music in them die away in the air. The gift was purely individual and momentary." And yet it was upon the possession of this gift, which had no future of any sort before it, that the Corinthians prided themselves most!

But even the nobler gifts of knowledge and prophecy were also to be "done away," done away by being swallowed up and absorbed in more complete knowledge and truer prophecy—as the twilight of morning is swallowed up in broad daylight, as the pools left on the beach at ebb tide are swallowed up in the fullness of the ocean when the tide comes sweeping back again.

"We know in part," says the apostle. That is true of every kind of knowledge. It is partial and fragmentary: it is never complete. It is perfectly true that the area of knowledge is being continually enlarged, inroads are constantly being made on the mystery that shuts us in on every side, men are forever pushing their explorations into the unknown. Never has the growth of knowledge been so rapid as in the past fifty years. And yet the men who know the most are the men who are most vividly conscious that they know only in part. As someone has said, it is only the second-year undergraduate who affects omniscience, and is cocksure and dogmatic. The real scholar is only too painfully aware of the limitations of his knowledge. He is confronted on every side by questions to which he can give no answer, by mysteries which he cannot solve. The apostle never said a truer word than this, "we know in part." In every department of science you will find men engaged in research work. And every bit of research work carried on at this moment in every laboratory under the sun proceeds on the assumption that we know only in part. If our knowledge were full and complete there would be no need for research. But the case stands today as Sir Isaac Newton felt it stood in his day—we pick up a few pebbles on the shore while the great ocean of knowledge spreads itself out before us untraversed, unexplored. We know only in part; that is why Michaelangelo said, when an old man, that he carried the schoolboy's satchel still. That is why J. R. Green said that he would die learning. But while the apostle recognizes that the knowledge is partial, he takes it for granted that it will grow—that as the result of thought and inquiry and research additions will continually be made to it. Patient investigation will wrest from the unknown its secrets, and knowledge will constantly become more complete. And what will be the result of this growing completeness of knowledge? The supersession of the old and less complete and less accurate knowledge. "When that which is perfect is come, that which is in part shall be done away." That is always happening—the less perfect is forever giving way to the more perfect. Look where you like, you see illustrations of this truth.

Take the lighting of our homes and streets: candles gave way to lamps, lamps to gas, and gas to electric light. Take our modes of travel: the stage coach gave way to the railway train and the old *Rocket* of George Stephenson has given place to the enormous express engines of today; the horse-drawn vehicle is giving way in our days to the motorcar, and perhaps before long the motorcar will give place to the airplane. Take the matter of shipping. In the old days men crossed the seas in boats driven by ranks of rowers; then came the long day of the sailing vessel; then came the day of the coal-burning steamer; and now the coal-burning steamer is giving place to the oil-burning steamer; and it may be that before very long that strange rotary craft, whose progress across the sea the whole world watched, will displace the steamer.

Take our manufactures. Men are constantly discovering new and better ways of doing things. They are forever inventing more efficient machinery. It is of no use for the manufacturer to go on with the old slow and ineffective machine once the newer and more efficient machine has been invented. If he does so he will soon be beaten in the fierce competitive struggle and will find himself in the Bankruptcy Court. There is nothing for it but ruthlessly to scrap the old machinery—when that which is perfect is come, that which is in part must be done away. This law operates not only in the realm of mechanics, but it operates just as surely in the realm of learning. The more complete is continually superseding the less complete. For centuries, for example, the Ptolemaic system which taught that the sun went round this earth, that regarded this earth as the center of the universe, held the field. Then came Copernicus with his theory that the earth went round the sun. It was obviously a theory which more truly and adequately accounted for the facts; once this more perfect theory had come the old partial inaccurate Ptolemaic theory had simply to pass away. Until comparatively recently the idea was held that the world was created in six days. Then the geologists read the story of the rocks, and the rocks spoke not of a world made in six days and some six thousand years old, the rocks spoke of a world that had taken millenniums and millenniums to become the world we know it. In the light of this newer and more accurate knowledge, the old and rather childlike ideas of the world's history have had to be given up. When the more perfect came, that which was in part was done away. Also until a time within the memory of living people it was held that all the creatures, including man, had always existed as they are today. They were created in the form we see them today. Then came Darwin with his *Origin of Species* and his theory of evolution. It suited the facts better than the old idea of special creation; and with most people who claim to be in any sense scholarly, evolution has taken the place of special creation. In the light of the newer and more accurate knowledge, that which was partial and inaccurate has passed away. New discovery is constantly making yesterday's knowledge obsolete. That is why, as Henry Drummond says, you can buy old editions of the great encyclopedias for a few pence. The knowledge they contain has passed away because fresh and more complete knowledge has come.

And all this is specially true in the realm of religious truth. That is how the knowledge of God has come—"bit by bit," as Moffatt expresses it. God of old, as the writer of the epistle to the Hebrews puts it, spoke unto the fathers in the prophets by divers portions and in divers manners. He revealed parts of His ways, and gave glimpses of His nature to this man and that. The revelation of God was progressive. There is a vast difference between the conception of God you get in the prophets and the psalms, and the conception of God you get in the earlier historical books. The Hebrews gradually emerged from belief in a God who was simply a tribal deity to belief in a God of all the earth exalted in righteousness. The old notion of a God who was one amongst many was superseded by the infinitely truer notion of one holy and living God. But the prophets and psalmists did not say the last word about God. Jesus says the last word. In Him the perfect revelation is given. He supersedes every psalmist and prophet. All that was true in their teaching is taken up and absorbed in the teaching of Jesus. But we do not go to them to know about God. We go to Him who was God manifest in the flesh. Prophets and psalmists as authorities upon God are out of date. When that which is perfect is come, that which is in part shall be done away. And ever since Christ came, knowledge has been growing. Not that we can ever outgrow Him. But we can grow in our understanding of Him. And that is what has been happening all down the centuries—the Spirit has been taking the things of Christ and revealing them to us; and with the growing understanding, religious ideas that once held sway are continually being superseded and discarded. Our conceptions of God, for example, have changed. The stern old Calvinistic conception of God as an arbitrary Sovereign has given place to the conception of Him as Father. The old ideas of atonement as a ransom paid to the Devil, or even as an offering to placate an angry God, have been superseded by truer views which see in the Cross the sacrifice of the Father as well as of the Son. Even the old ideas about "last things" are changing, and a sermon like that of Jonathan Edwards, "Sinners in the Hands of an Angry God," which produced such tremendous effects when it was preached, would leave men cold today. Men have moved away from the ideas on which that sermon was based. Newer and more perfect views have come, and so, that which was in part has just passed away. We know in part. A sentence like that ought to warn us against dogmatism and against thinking or speaking as if our views on religious truth were absolutely accurate, and we were therefore free to condemn those who differ from us. Men who have been branded as heretics in their day have been revealed by history to be just pioneers of larger truths. The fact that we know only in part ought to beget within us the open mind, just because we know there is still more light and truth to break forth from God's Word, and our present knowledge may be itself made obsolete by such new light and truth. "We know in part," says the apostle, "and we prophesy in part." The two things hang together; the one is the result and consequence of the other. Partial knowledge means, inevitably, partial prophecy. For taking prophecy as being the ancient equivalent of our preaching—preaching is always the declaration of what a man knows. "That which we have seen with our eyes, that which we beheld and our hands handled concerning the Word of

Life, that declare we unto you." But just because knowledge grows, prophecy will vary. We know more than our fathers did, therefore the kind of preaching in which they indulged is no longer possible to us today. We cannot proceed from their assumptions. Truer views of the Bible, for example, have come to us. We cannot argue as they argued, using the Bible as an armory of proof texts and treating it as if every part of it were of equal authority. With the larger knowledge the old style of preaching has passed away. Even in the case of the individual person, knowledge grows and therefore preaching alters. I am quite conscious that my preaching is very different from what it was thirty-six years ago when I began my ministry. And the change is not simply one of style, but of accent and emphasis, and even of substance. I laid the emphasis when I began on the demands God makes of men. I lay the emphasis in these days on what God in Christ has done for me. And the reason for the difference is that in the intervening years I have enlarged my knowledge—not simply my knowledge of books, but my knowledge of men, of human life, of the needs and sorrows, the sins and tragedies of my fellow creatures. And the larger knowledge has brought a different kind of preaching, a preaching I would fain believe that is nearer to the spirit of the New Testament. We prophesy in part, but as more perfect knowledge comes, that which is in part is done away.

The apostle further illustrates his theme by the change that comes over thought and speech and belief as the human creature progresses from childhood to manhood. "When I was a child, I spake as a child, I felt as a child, I thought [or, I reasoned] as a child; now that I am become a man, I have put away childish things." "When I was a child, I spake as a child." The child, according to the psychologists, awakes to self-consciousness at the age of three. It realizes itself as a self then, and begins from its sense impressions to form its own conceptions of the world. But it isn't the world as we older people know it. Every child is an Alice in Wonderland and lives in a world of fantasy and imagination—a world peopled by elves and fairies and angels. It is not the real world, but we would not have the child anything but the fanciful creature he is. We like the child to speak and think as a child. We do not want to see an old head on young shoulders. That was the tragedy of Coleridge's life—he never was a child. But if we do not want to see an old head on young shoulders, we as little like to see a child's head on old shoulders. There are some people who, like Peter Pan, never seem to grow up; but we do not admire them. Everything is beautiful in its time, but a person who is a man in years while still a child in mind and habit is just a monstrosity. But speaking generally, as childhood merges into youth, and youth into adult life, we shed our childish methods of speech and of thought because we are with advancing years better able to grasp the realities of things. "When I became a man, I put away childish things." And there is a similar growth from childhood to manhood in Christian knowledge and experience. There are some people who are mere babes in Christ, there are others who are full-grown men. The same person begins by being a babe fed with milk, but develops into a man in Christ who can be fed with meat. There is therefore of necessity something partial and temporary about all forms of knowledge and prophecy. The kind of teaching that suits one age of the world's life does not suit another; the kind of teaching that suits a man at one stage of his spiritual development does not suit him at another. There is a constant supervision of outgrown and superseded statements of truth. "When I became a man, I put away childish things."

And now I come to the verse with which the apostle winds up this parenthesis about the temporary character of these gifts of knowledge and prophecy because new accessories of knowledge are constantly making the old knowledge obsolete. I think in this verse the apostle implies that though knowledge may grow from more to more, it will to the very end, so far as this earth is concerned, remain incomplete. It is only in the next world that fullness of knowledge will be ours. The contrast in verse 12 is really a contrast between this world and the next; between the condition of Christ's people here on earth, and the condition of the same people when perfected and glorified.

The condition of Christ's people here is one of broken vision and partial knowledge. "For now we see in a mirror, darkly." To understand and appreciate the figure we must remember that the mirrors of the ancient days were not like ours. Glass mirrors with quicksilver at the back didn't make their appearance till the thirteenth century. Ancient mirrors were made of polished metal either bronze or silver. Corinth was famous for the manufacture of these mirrors. But it needs no pointing out that these metal mirrors did not reflect every line and feature truly as our modern mirrors do. They reflected the object, but the lines were more or less blurred and uncertain.

Some translate the words, "through a glass," the figure in that case being of a man peering in through a window—ancient windows again being made not of clear glass, but of semitranslucent talc, the result being that the figures seen within appeared dim and vague. "In a mirror" is almost certainly the right translation, but in either case the suggestion is the same, that of wavering and uncertain vision. And to place his meaning beyond all doubt the apostle adds: "Now we see in a mirror, darkly," or rather, "in a riddle." We see, but what we see often puzzles and perplexes us. We see, and yet we have all sorts of problems and difficulties. "We see in a mirror, in a riddle." It is a wonderfully expressive description of the kind of knowledge we have down here. Of course, at this point the apostle is thinking of our knowledge of God. God has revealed Himself in many ways to us and we catch glimpses of Him, but it is in a riddle—vaguely and uncertainly we see Him.

We see Him in nature in the fresh beauty of the spring, in the pearly gray of the dawn, in the glory of the sunset. We are in the mood often to say, "The earth is full of the goodness of the Lord and the heavens declare His glory." And then with a jolt we remember there are ugly and terrible things in nature. There are venomous reptiles as well as faithful animals like the dog; there are hawks as well as larks; there are vultures as well as linnets; there are tornadoes and earthquakes as well as summer suns and smiling seas. And when some natural catastrophe lays Tokyo in ruins, and swallows up in sudden death thousands of human beings, we are sorely puzzled to reconcile it with our conception of God. We do not give up our faith; we see God, but it is in a mirror, in a riddle.

We see God in history. Over long stretches of time it is impossible to question the fact that God is at work. Life is not meaningless and purposeless. There's a Divinity that shapes our ends. But it is desperately difficult sometimes to see Him, much less to understand Him. The Old Testament is full of the complaints and moans of men who only saw God in a mirror, in a riddle. Indeed, they were more often conscious of the riddle than of the vision. Take Job for illustration. He held to his faith in God. "Even though He slay me, yet will I trust Him." But he was puzzled and perplexed by God's dealings almost to the point of rebellion and despair. His speech is compact of doubt and question and challenge. He saw dimly and uncertainly. God was a riddle to

him. And so it is still. We believe in Providence. We think we can
see signs of God's working. But things are often strangely baffling
and puzzling. They suggest questions we cannot answer and raise
doubts we cannot solve. Don't you remember, for example, how
people were staggered in those dark years of war—how they
wondered why God didn't bring the war to an end, and how they
wondered too that He allowed even for a single instant wrong to
get the upper hand? It was all hard to reconcile with faith in a
loving and righteous God. And there are happenings in our
individual lives just as puzzling. This very week I have been with
one of our people who for months has been suffering almost
incessant torturing pain. She wonders why God permits it. We
wonder too. "Now we see in a mirror, in a riddle."

We see God in the Bible. We see Him there more clearly than
anywhere else. Because in it we see through the eyes of men who
were granted clearer vision than is granted to ordinary mortals. But
even in the Bible we are conscious of the uncertainty of our
knowledge. For prophets and psalmists themselves saw in a mirror.
They had their doubts and difficulties and challenges, and the
shadows of them fall across their pages. Even the best of them saw
in a mirror, in a riddle. We see God most clearly of all in Christ.
And yet in Christ there are many things we do not clearly understand.
And in the full light of His revelation there are things we do not
clearly see. Indeed, while from one point of view Christ is the
revelation of God, from another point of view it is true to say (in the
words of the old hymn) that "it is veiled in flesh," we see the
Godhead "veiled"—in a mirror, in a riddle. Jesus could not even
explain Himself entirely and completely. "I have many things to say
unto you, but ye cannot bear them now." That is the characteristic
of our knowledge of God and His love and grace—we see in a
mirror, in a riddle!

But our knowledge is not to remain always broken and imperfect.
"For now we see in a mirror darkly—but then face to face." Face-
to-face—with no shadow or cloud between. We shall see not some
dim and wavering reflection of God, but God Himself in all His
glory and grace. Every perplexity will have vanished, every problem
will have been solved, all doubts and questionings will have clean
gone. We shall see Him face-to-face. This is the beatific vision
which brings perfect joy to the soul. I can understand Faber crying
out,

> What rapture will it be,
> Prostrate before Thy throne to lie,
> And gaze and gaze on Thee.

Perfect vision and fullness of knowledge! "Then shall I know even as also I have been known." I shall know fully—that is the meaning of the word—just as I have been fully known. "What I do thou knowest not now," said Jesus, "but thou shalt know hereafter." Heaven is the place where all our questions are going to be answered and all our doubts and challenges met. We shall know the why and wherefore of God's dealings with us. We shall see then how God always and in everything is perfect love. That is one of the blessings heaven is going to bring with it, or rather it would be better to say that is part of the blessedness of heaven—to see and to know. The crooked shall be made straight, and the rough places plain, and the glory of the Lord shall be revealed. That is the prospect wherewith we can comfort and sustain our souls when events perplex and trouble us, and we cannot understand. One day we shall see God face-to-face, one day we shall know fully even as we are fully known, and then we shall joyfully confess that God did all things well.

> So faith and patience! wait awhile
> Not doubting, not in fear:
> For soon in heaven my Father's smile
> Shall render all things clear.

CHAPTER TEN

The Supremacy of Love

But now abideth faith, hope, love, these three; and the
greatest of these is love.   *—1 Corinthians 13:13*

With this simple but almost fathomless sentence the apostle brings this exquisite hymn to a finish. He ends it on the top note. He keeps his most splendid chord for the last. Everything he has said hitherto culminates in the climax of this final statement. In the verses immediately preceding he has been asserting the superiority of love over the gifts of tongues and prophecy and knowledge—the gifts on which the Corinthians plumed and prided themselves—on the ground that, while these gifts were transient and temporary, love was permanent. "Love never faileth, but whether there be prophecies, they shall be done away; whether there be tongues, they shall cease; whether there be knowledge, it shall be done away." But in this verse Paul says something about love more wonderful still; he makes a claim for it more daring still. Not only is love better than such transient things as prophecy and tongues and knowledge, but of the permanent and abiding things love is the greatest and the best. For love is not the only thing that abides. Faith abides, and hope abides as well. Now abideth faith, hope, love; but the greatest of these— even of these supreme and vital things—the greatest of these is love.

In that beautiful little booklet in which Henry Drummond expounds this chapter, he speaks of love as "the greatest thing in the world." Of course, it is that. But that description of it is an understatement. It falls short of the truth. Love is not only the greatest thing in the world, it is also the greatest thing in heaven; it is not only the greatest thing in time, it is also the greatest thing in eternity. "Now abideth faith, hope, love, these three; and the greatest of these is love."

It seems something like sacrilege to begin to examine critically a verse like this, but I should not be quite honest if I did not at least let you know that a whole school of commentators, beginning with Chrysostom, put a rather different construction upon the verse from that which is commonly received. They treat that word *Now* with which the verse opens as being not the "now" of logic, but the "now" of time. Now in this present time, in this temporal sphere, there are three abiding things—faith, hope and love. But in the eternal world faith and hope will disappear; there will be no further occasion for their exercise. But love will live on through all eternity. Love is superior even to faith and hope, for they will cease; but love, as Dr. Edwards says, "will survive every catastrophe." It is the interpretation embodied in that verse of our familiar hymn:

> Faith will vanish into sight;
> Hope be emptied in delight.
> Love in heaven will shine more bright,
>   Therefore give us love.

But though a great many scholars favor that interpretation, I am quite persuaded that the ordinary interpretation is the right one. I find it quite impossible to think that the word *abideth* when applied to faith and hope means "abideth for a time"; but that when applied to love it means "abideth forever." This is what Paul says: "Now abideth faith, hope, love." So far as the abiding is concerned, these three graces stand on the same plane. What "abiding" means for any one of them, it means for all three of them. Faith, hope, love are alike in this—that they are all permanent. But someone may say, "What room is there for faith and hope in heaven?" What room is there for faith? Here we have to walk by faith, not by sight. We have to take many things on trust. We have to believe that God is at work, though we cannot behold Him. We have to believe that all things work together for good, though they seem to us to be hopelessly tangled and awry. We have to believe that God is love, though oftentimes things look very unlike it. But what room is there for faith in heaven? What did that last verse say, Now we see in a mirror—in a riddle—but then face-to-face; now I know in part, but then I shall fully know, even as also I have been fully known. We shall see—face-to-face—without the smallest wisp of cloud or shred of mist to dim our vision! There will be no longer any riddles to perplex and baffle us. We shall know! We shall know completely; our agonized whys and wherefores will get their answers there. Isn't that a large element in the blessedness of heaven—that the crooked will be made straight and the rough place plain, and that the glory of the Lord will be fully revealed? What room is there left for faith in that land where the beatific vision will be ours? And what room is there for hope? Does not hope by its very nature seem to argue an imperfect world? That is how the case stands with us down here—we hope for things, but we do not always achieve them. Perhaps it would be truer to say that we never completely realize them. A certain element of disappointment seems to be inseparable from this human life of ours. We hope to accomplish certain tasks, and they are not half finished when the end comes. We hope to reach a certain height of character, and we are not halfway up the hill when the night falls. We are all of us like David in this respect—it is in our minds to do great things, but the great things never get done. And sometimes the disappointments are bitter and tragic. Think, for example, of the hopes that lie dashed and broken in the untimely graves of youth—the hopes for England, for example, that lie buried in the graves of Rupert Brooke and young Gladstone and the Grenfells; of the hopes innumerable parents cherished for their lads which the brutal hand of sudden death nipped in the very bud. Hope is a bittersweet kind of thing. We could not live without it, but disappointment is its twin sister, and it argues in its very nature an uncertain life and an imperfect world. But what room is there for hope in heaven? For is not that how we picture heaven—as the place of realization and achievement? What does our old hymn say?

> There shall we feel and see and know,
> All we desired or hoped below.

"All we desired or hoped"! Is not that how we comfort ourselves in face of the shattering of our hopes for our children snatched from us in their youth—that all the promise that was in them will get its chance in heaven? "On the earth the broken arcs, in heaven the perfect round." Is not that how we comfort ourselves in face of our own imperfections and shortcomings, in face of our manifold failures and falls—falls which lay us in the very dust of shame—that in heaven we shall be completely freed from every root and fiber of sin; and that there, at last, we shall be what we want to be? Does not this Book tell us that in that day we shall be like our Lord, for we shall see Him as He is? Well, what will there be to wish for after that? What place is there for hope in heaven?

And yet here is the apostle declaring categorically that not love only, but faith and hope also, are abiding things. It is not love alone that "never faileth," faith and hope never fail either. They have their place in the life of heaven. They are not transient and temporary things like prophecy and tongues. They are permanent graces of the soul. "Now abideth faith, hope, love—these three." Can we understand how this should be? Well, it behooves a man to talk very diffidently when he comes to speak of conditions in the life to come, for eye hath not seen nor ear heard, neither have entered into the mind of man the things which God has prepared for them that love Him. But I think we may find certain clues which—if we follow them—will help us to understand why Paul numbers faith and hope among the abiding things.

Let me once again begin with faith. If we understand faith to be a certain act of the intellect by which we believe in certain promises on the ground of our belief in the Promiser (which was Chrysostom's notion of faith), then, of course, faith ceases when the promises are fulfilled. Or, if we understand faith as an intellectual assent to a certain scheme of doctrine (which is an idea of faith not unfamiliar in Protestant circles), then again faith ceases because in the clear light of heaven our stumbling conceptions of truth will be swallowed up in the immediate perception of the truth itself. But is that the real meaning of faith? Does not faith in its essence mean this—trust in God, the confidence of the soul in God, the clinging of the soul to God? When we say that we walk by faith not by sight, is not that what we mean, that we trust God though we cannot see Him? We believe that in the deepest darkness He is at work, though we cannot behold Him. We stake everything on the belief that He is love, even though events challenge and seem to deny our faith. "Even though He slay me yet will I trust Him." Well, won't there be room for faith in that sense of trust, "the clinging of the heart to God and to a living, personal Christ," as Dr. Edwards puts it, in the life of heaven? Will faith as a matter of fact not flourish more vigorously than ever? What our clear vision of God, our sight of Him face-to-face will do, is not to do away with faith but to intensify it. Down here faith has often a struggle for life. "Faith and unfaith can ne'er be equal powers," says Tennyson. No, perhaps not! But often, in actual experience, there is very little in it, on the balance. We are so perplexed and troubled, so puzzled and baffled by the tangled providences of life that faith almost lapses into unfaith and the best prayer we can offer is "Lord, I believe, help thou mine unbelief." But up yonder we shall see the meaning of things. We shall see how, all through, God has been thinking on us for our good. We shall see how trustworthy He is. And as a result of our clearer vision of God our hearts will cling to Him with a more perfect trust, with a confidence uncheckered by any shadow of doubt. The difference between earth and heaven is the difference between a halting and hesitating faith and a glad and triumphant faith. But the life yonder, as here, will be one of clinging trust in God. "Now abideth faith."

And what about hope? I have found reason for the permanence of faith in the fact that the relation between man and God will always be that of joyful and adoring trust. I find the reason for the permanence of hope in the nature of that heaven-life itself. We make a mistake if we think of all the denizens of heaven as being on the same level. "One star differeth from another star in glory," says St. Paul. "So also," he adds, "is the resurrection of the dead." There are differences in heaven, differences of attainment and glory. There are some who are scarcely saved, and there are some who have an abundant entrance into the heavenly habitations. And this fact of difference in attainment is quite compatible with the perfect blessedness of all. Each has all the blessedness he can contain. There is fullness of joy for all, though the capacity for joy may vary in each case. And just as there are differences between the inhabitants of heaven, so there are differences in the same person at different stages. There is progress even in heaven. Our condition is not fixed forever once we reach there. "In My Father's house," said Jesus, "there are many mansions." "Resting places," the word really means, and it refers to those stations on the great roads where travelers could get rest and refreshment before proceeding on their journey.

The notions both of repose and progress, says Bishop Westcott, are in the word. We shall be moving on, so to speak, from one resting place to another. And this idea of progress, this again, is in no way inconsistent with perfection. For just exactly as in this human life of ours a person may be perfect as a child, and then perfect as a youth, and finally perfect as a man, so in the next world we may be continually growing and making progress and yet be perfect at each stage. And, as Dr. Edwards says, so long as progress is possible, hope has not ceased.

I suppose that in heaven, as here on earth, we shall be limited creatures. And limited creatures will always find something fresh to learn about the infinite God. With all saints we shall be forever seeking to apprehend what is the breadth and length and depth and height of the love of God. That is a task that will occupy us through all eternity, and with every fresh discovery of that love our perfection will become a deeper, fuller, and richer thing.

I talked with a devoted member of this church the other day, and she found great comfort in this thought of progress. She felt so unworthy and sinful that she felt she needed some long process of purification before she was fit for the presence of God. But in process of time she dared to hope even that final felicity might be hers. I think she forgot two things—first of all, that we are to be completely purged from our sins; and, secondly, she forgot that it is love that qualifies for the vision. Every one that loveth is born of God. The progress of heaven is not that we are gradually emancipated from sin and gradually gain the vision of God's face, but that as we contemplate God's love we grow in our knowledge of God and enter upon an ever-enlarging life in Him. But the progress is sure. The perfection of today will merge into the larger perfection of tomorrow. There is always something richer and better to look for. There is room for hope in the life of heaven. As Mr. Percy Ainsworth puts it: "Faith and hope will not cease to live when they no longer have to fight for their life. They are not mere adjuncts of human life. They are the fundamental terms of our personal existence and the eternal conditions of our relationship with God, and they must abide so long as God and the soul abide." So faith and hope, as well as love, are permanent and abiding things. They have their place in the life of heaven. "Now abideth faith, hope, love, these three," and only these three. And then the apostle adds these words: "and the greatest of these is love." Love is not simply greater than transient and temporary gifts like prophecy and tongues; it is greater than these abiding graces of the soul—faith and hope. It is the greatest thing in heaven itself. After letting his mind dwell on the various gifts on which the members of the church militant prided themselves, and finding among them nothing comparable to love, he lifts his eyes to the contemplation of the saints in glory, and he finds that love still holds pride of place, "the greatest of these is love."

Now can we see why love is greater than either faith or hope? I am going to mention two considerations. Dr. Edwards says that St. Paul does not tell us why love is greater than faith and hope. St. Paul, he says, only opens the door. To enter was reserved for St. John. But even in this very chapter the apostle gives us a hint as to why love is better than either faith or hope.

The Supremacy of Love

(1) Without love, faith and hope are themselves imperfect. He has said as much as that in plain language about faith. "If I have all faith so as to remove mountains and have not love . . . I am nothing." There is a kind of faith which hasn't very much love in it. It is the kind of faith which lays hold of the merits of Christ, but has nothing in it of a spontaneous and eager delight in God. And there is a kind of hope which hasn't very much love in it. The hope which animates some Christian people is like that very materialistic hope that possessed the hearts of the first disciples, and which prompted Peter one day to say, "Lo, we have left all and followed Thee, what then shall we get?" What they hope for is reward or, at any rate, escape from punishment. But such faith and such hope are poor and imperfect things. Both need love for their perfection. Love changes faith from trust in Christ's merits into an enthusiastic devotion to Christ Himself. Love transforms hope from hope of reward into hope of likeness to Christ, and blessed union with Him. Love is a greater thing than either faith or hope, because without love faith and hope are themselves poor and imperfect things.

So far Paul takes us in this chapter. But it is John who supplies us with the final reason why love is greater than either faith or hope.

(2) Love is the divine grace. You cannot describe God in terms of faith or hope. "God, the all-knowing, does not believe. God, the all-possessing, does not hope." But you can describe God in terms of love. Indeed, those are the only terms in which you can describe Him. God is love. Power, wisdom, omnipresence—those are

attributes of God. But love is His very nature. That is the truth blazoned for us in the Cross of Jesus. We might have been doubtful of it but for that final and subduing revelation. God gave His Son to death and shame for love. Faith and hope are eternal things, inasmuch as they are the abiding conditions of our relationship with God, but when we love we share God's very life. "Faith and hope are means to an end; love is the end itself." Faith and hope link us to the life of God, but love is that life itself. We enter into the very life of God, and union with God becomes a blessed reality when we love. For God is love, and every one that loveth is born of God and knoweth God. That is why the apostle says, "Now abideth faith, hope, love, these three; and the greatest of these is love."

"The greatest thing in the world," says Henry Drummond. Of course it is that. It is the chief spring of such happiness as we enjoy down here. I do not say that there are not other thing such as the glory of the physical world in which we live, and the companionship of books, and the delights of music and art—that add to the richness and fullness of life. But love is the abiding source of our happiness and peace. It is love—the love of father and mother, and wife and child, and friend that makes life worth having. Without love, life is not a boon but a burden. "If a man have no friend"—it is Bacon, I think, who says it—"he may quit the stage." He probably will quit the stage. A man has no hold on life when love is gone. Analyse your own feelings and see if this is not so. "Why," asks Drummond, "do you want to live tomorrow? It is because there is someone who loves you and whom you want to see tomorrow and be with and love back." But who would want to live if in the wide world we had neither love nor friend? So that in the last analysis, as Drummond says, love is life, and we live only while we love. But so long as we have love, life is worthwhile. As we grow old, the senses which are the gateways through which other enjoyments reach us, often fail. The eyes give out and we can be no longer ravished by the glories of nature; hearing becomes dull and we can no longer be charmed by music and song. But old people for whom life has been in that way limited and curtailed still find it worthwhile—for though sight is gone and hearing is gone, love is still left. It is in very truth, without controversy or dispute, the greatest thing in the world. And if we only knew it, love is the healing of our world's hurt. It is not only the fountain of happiness for the individual life; it is the only possible means of quietness and peace for our world. It is not by new arrangements and changes of method we are going to bring peace and goodwill back to our disordered world, but by a change of spirit. We may make what changes of method and of organization we please, but so long as we have the same selfish spirit, strife and division, unrest and discontent will be with us still. But though our methods and our organization remained as they are, confessedly imperfect, to say the least—if only we had, filling the hearts of men, this love which envieth not, which beareth, hopeth, and believeth all things, and which never fails, love by itself as by a stroke of a magician's wand would present us with the new world.

Love is not only the best thing in life, and the healing of the world's hurt, it is the Alpha and Omega of religion. You can sum up religion in terms of love. For what is the final and ultimate source of this Christian faith of ours? What is its primal and original fount? Why, the infinite love of God. "God so loved the world." Everything begins with that uncreated and eternal love. But for that love there would have been for lost and wayward men no redemption or salvation at all. And when does that salvation provided by the uncreated love of God become a reality in individual experience? When does religion begin in you and me? When love for God wakens in these hearts of ours. When looking into the face of Jesus—that torn and scarred visage—we say with Peter, "Lord, thou knowest all things, thou knowest that I love thee." And how does religion show itself? What is its practical effect in life? And again I say, Love. By this know we that we have passed out of death into life—because we love the brethren. Pure and undefiled religion before God and the Father is this: to visit the fatherless and widows in their affliction and to keep oneself unspotted from the world. We are sometimes half inclined to identify religion with creeds and doctrines, and rites and ceremonies. We are wrong there. Creeds and doctrines, rites and ceremonies are not of the essence of religion. But you can sum religion up in terms of love. It begins in eternity with the love of God; it starts in you and me, when our love responds to that mighty love of God; and it reveals itself in the loving life.

"The greatest thing in the world"? Yes, it is that. But it is more than that. It is the greatest thing in heaven as well. Of all the abiding things, love is supreme. "Now abideth faith, hope, love, these three; and the greatest of these is love." It is the very life of heaven, for it is the nature of God Himself. Heaven is the abode of the loving.

Love is the qualification for entrance, and the selfish and unloving find no admittance. The test of entrance into the Celestial City, as Drummond puts it, "is not religiousness, but love. Not what I have done, not what I have believed, not what I have achieved, but how I have discharged the common charities of life." "Come, ye blessed, inherit the kingdom prepared for you from the foundation of the world." Who are these people? They are just the loving—the people who fed the hungry and clothed the naked, and visited the sick, and who out of sheer love went about doing good. We all want to win home to that blessed country at the finish. Well, have you got love? It is of no use talking about your orthodoxy and your church membership and the rest of it. You will not be asked questions about those things—but have you got love, this sacred love for God and man that reveals itself in a loving life? You may have faith so as to remove mountains, yet if you have no love be nothing at all. Love is the one thing needful. It is the very spirit of Jesus. And if we have not the spirit of Christ we are none of His. If you have not got it, do you desire it? How can love be got? Where can love be kindled? I will tell you. At the Cross of Jesus. Gaze at that Cross long enough and realize that it was for you He hung and suffered there—and love will be born. The love of Christ will constrain you, once you realize that the Son of God loved you and gave Himself up for you.

Great Sermons by Great Pulpiteers

FRANK W. BOREHAM

Life Verses #1—A Bunch of Everlastings
ISBN 0-8254-2167-5   192 pp.   (pb)

Life Verses #2—A Handful of Stars
ISBN 0-8254-2169-1   208 pp.   (pb)

Life Verses #3—A Casket of Cameos
ISBN 0-8254-2168-3   208 pp.   (pb)

Life Verses #4—A Bundle of Torches
ISBN 0-8254-2165-9   256 pp.   (pb)

Life Verses #5—A Temple of Topaz
ISBN 0-8254-2166-7   272 pp.   (pb)

The Luggage of Life
ISBN 0-8254-2164-0   256 pp.   (pb)

Mountains in the Mist
ISBN 0-8254-2163-2   288 pp.   (pb)

CHARLES G. FINNEY

God's Love for a Sinning World
ISBN 0-8254-2620-0   122 pp.   (pb)

The Guilt of Sin
ISBN 0-8254-2616-2   124 pp.   (pb)

Prevailing Prayer
ISBN 0-8254-2603-0   66 pp.   (pb)

So Great Salvation
ISBN 0-8254-2621-9   128 pp.   (pb)

True and False Repentence
ISBN 0-8254-2617-0   122pp.   (pb)

True Saints
ISBN 0-8254-2622-7   120 pp.   (pb)

True Submission
ISBN 0-8254-2618-9   128 pp.   (pb)

Victory Over the World
ISBN 0-8254-2619-7   124 pp.   (pb)

J. D. JONES

The Apostles of Jesus
ISBN 0-8254-2971-4   144 pp.   (pb)

CLARENCE E. MACARTNEY

Chariots of Fire
ISBN 0-8254-3274-x   160 pp.   (pb)

The Faith Once Delivered
ISBN 0-8254-3281-4   144 pp.   (pb)

Great Women of the Bible
ISBN 0-8254-3268-5   160 pp.   (pb)